Clumsy Construction
in Mark's Gospel

A Critique of Form-
and Redaktionsgeschichte

John C. Meagher

The Edwin Mellen Press
New York and Toronto

Toronto Studies in Theology, Volume Three

The Edwin Mellen Press
Suite 918
225 West 34th Street
New York, New York 10001

Library of Congress Cataloging Number 79-66373

ISBN 0-88946-876-1

Toronto Studies in Theology, ISBN 0-88946-975X

Printed in the United States of America

For Richard J. Schoeck:

> not only a scholar in himself, but the
> cause that scholarship is in others;
>
> not only a gentleman, but a lesson in
> "Bountee, Gentilesse, and Courtesye."

CONTENTS

PREFACE

The purpose of this book is to suggest a
new perspective for reading the Gospel of Mark,
and a new perspective for understanding the formation of the first three Gospels in general.

There are, of course, many ways of reading
the Gospels. My undertaking is directed at the
pattern of reading that obtains almost universally in the academic world: the scientific criticism of the Gospels. The adjective still rings a
bit oddly in the English speaker's ear. "Science"
readily conjures up images of the laboratory, but
not of the library or the private study. German
is bolder, and forthrightly applies the term
Wissenschaft to whatever forms of systematic ra-
tional inquiry are appropriate to the material at
hand, whether or not they allow of experiment or
quantification. The English speaking world has
not yet made that generalization of the term.
My faculty in the University of Toronto is enti-
tled "Arts and Science," and there is little doubt
in anyone's mind that when we study the Gospels,
we do so according to the former rubric, not the
latter. This disparity undoubtedly has some

connection with the fact that the advanced rigorous study of the Gospels has, over the last few generations, developed far more through German scholarship than through any other, or combination of other, investigations. The psychology of science is different from the psychology of art. It tends to promote confidence, rigor, stability, and a commitment to cumulative accomplishment. It has accordingly brought the study of the Gospels to a remarkably refined and steady condition.

Arts and sciences alike are subject to a certain inertia of achievement. Successful styles of proceeding tend to entrench themselves, and are not easily dislodged by proffered alternatives. But such changes come about far more slowly in science than in art, mainly because the scientist tends to suppose that his presuppositions are progressively proved *true,* while the artist tends to settle for finding his presuppositions *effective.* Reflective scientists will acknowledge that the difference fades under close scrutiny: presuppositions are presuppositions, and cannot themselves be verified; all science is founded on an art of investigation that is no less an art for producing useful and consistent results. Those results do not prove the truth of the presuppositions, merely their constant and effective presence.

Underlying the modern scientific study of the Gospels are some important presuppositions about the ways in which the materials of the Gospels were begotten, shaped, transmitted, changed, and eventually written down. The evidences we have for the oral tradition underlying the written Gospels are to be found in the written Gospels themselves: by the nature of the case, oral tradition as such does not leave the sort of permanent record by which it may be directly studied. Hence it comes that the modern image of pre-Gospel oral tradition is not, and cannot, be founded on direct empirical evidence, but only on inference and presupposition. I shall argue in the first part of this book that a good look at a live oral tradition in our own time must raise deep and serious questions about the adequacy of the model of oral tradition on which contemporary Gospel-study is based—that the key inferences are doubtful validity and the governing presuppositions are ill-founded. A curved surface, observed from above at a distance, seems flat, and able to be treated according to the rules of Euclidean plane geometry. But in fact the curvature makes all the difference: the Euclidean axioms will not hold, will not tell the truth about the surface's behavior. Observing the early Christian oral tradition from a distance, and through the limits of written texts, modern Gos-

pel criticism has formulated a set of axioms not
from the evidence alone but from unwarranted
presuppositions about how that evidence came to
be. Modern science has found that Euclidean
axioms are not aptly applicable to the physical
world in which we live. The matter is testable
by experiment. We cannot test the Gospels ex-
perimentally, but we can observe analogous phenomena in our own time—and I believe, and will
try to show, that when we do so we ought to conclude that we should not accept as adequate the
axioms inferred from and applied to the Gospel
evidences by modern criticism. There is likely
to be a curvature which they cannot handle. This
cannot be proved; but it can be shown to be probable. Its probability invites a different way
of reading, analyzing, inferring, and reconstructing what lies behind and within the Gospel
texts.

This book is an essay, in the ancient technical sense of the word—an attempt, a sketch of
possibilities, a trial balloon. I acknowledge
this at the outset not to plead for critical
mercy, but quite the contrary, to beg for the
kind of thoughtful hearing that will mete out
critical justice. The views and arguments and
interpretive analyses presented herein have consistently been found "interesting," sometimes
persuasive, by the circles of scholars to whom I

have offered them on previous occasions. But I
have found it more difficult, on those occasions,
to establish a clear realization that if I am
right in these matters, then some other received
notions are importantly wrong. The book is brief,
and according to the prevailing critical assumptions it is unorthodox. But it says enough, I
believe, to make it possible for the reader to
grasp and assess my proposal, and to see what its
implications are on a larger scale or in more
thorough application than I here attempt. Its
unorthodoxy is of course part of its point, and
may not legitimately be taken as grounds for
finding it unpersuasive: it means to challenge
a critical orthodoxy to which it therefore cannot conform. If it does not persuade, I hope
that I will find out why. If it persuades, I
hope that it will not then be classified as "interesting" and set aside. This is a serious attempt, a sketch of potentially important possibilities, a trial balloon suggesting a considerable change in the weather.

I would like to offer my thanks to the
Journal of the American ACademy of Religion,
publisher of an earlier version of the first
part of this book; to Norman Petersen, whose critical comments on a still earlier version,
routinely and anonymously forwarded by *JAAR,*
were of great help in clarifying my thoughts and

procedures; Anne Adams, who called my attention
to an important piece of supporting evidence;
various friends and colleagues (here unnamed
for their protection) who inadvertently provided
needed examples for the first chapter; and various members of the Institute of Christian
Thought, especially Rosann Catalano, John Klop-
penborg, and Mary Ann Hinsdale, for memorable
varieties of help and support. And Herb Richardson
whose generous readiness to take a chance I have
happily admired for more than twenty years.

                          Toronto

                          The Feast of St. Mark, 197

CLUMSY CONSTRUCTION

IN

MARK'S GOSPEL

A CRITIQUE OF FORM-

AND

REDAKTIONSGESCHICHTE

CHAPTER ONE

FORM, REDACTION, AND
ORDINARY CLUMSINESS

Although some non-literate cultures still survive here and there, you do not belong to one. You probably have to trace your family back for several generations before you find an ancestor who did. As New Testament scholars have consistently reminded us, the cultural world of the Gospels' formation was of another order. The Gospels are the product of a culture that shepherded an oral tradition through paths of development alien to our literary minds, paths that can be known to us only by indirect inference.

In order to understand the formation of the Gospels with some degree of accuracy, we must somehow reconstruct what an oral tradition is like, however obliquely and artificially we may be constrained to do it. It is commonly recognized that we do not participate directly in such a process, but that we have useful ac-

cess to other contemporary cultures that do, as
well as to the records of the last preliterary
phases of our own culture. Hence the hearten-
ing and typical observations of a book recently
published:

> It is possible to learn a great
> deal about an oral period by
> studying the characteristics of
> oral traditions which lie close
> to our own time. There are
> living traditions of oral ma-
> terials still available in some
> cultures, and in our own some
> materials have only recently
> been reduced to writing, such
> as fairy tales, nursery rhymes,
> folk songs, and folk tales.[2]

Evidently, "recently" and "close to our own
time" are to be interpreted broadly, and mean
here something in the order of a century since
our culture participated in a live oral tradition. Such an assumption has become a scholarly commonplace.

But the fact of the matter is that the
world of oral tradition is not necessarily as
foreign to the direct experience of contemporary scholars as is often implied—at least to
scholars with a sense of humor. For despite
the domination of the written word over the content and habits of our culture, there is one
fresh stream of oral tradition that still flows
through it and has scarcely begun to mix with

the brackish waters of literariness: joke-telling. I submit that this enduring tradition
provides a fruitful analogue to the process by
which the Synoptic gospel-tradition was preserved and developed, and that a considered reflection on its nature and habits would be a
usefully perspective-giving and corrective way
of achieving a more balanced and accurate version of form criticism, and would illuminate
redaction criticism as well.

I. JOKES

The oral tradition of joke-telling is
generally familiar. There is hardly anyone
who has not participated in it. All its techniques are part of the public heritage, and we
apply them regularly, and hear them applied by
others, not only to pass stories on but to
adapt them to topical interests, make them more
entertaining, sharpen the point of their humor.
Enough such stories have been written down more
or less successfully to permit a future scholar,
when the living tradition is dead, to fancy that
he might be able to codify the ways in which
stories were thus enhanced, and use the results
as a way of reconstructing the histories of
stories once in current circulation.

But the resulting theoretical and ab-
stract history would be very unlike the real

history. For one thing, three surviving examples of a tale would give only the illusion of
perspective, and would reveal neither the dozen
other ways it was being told during its life-
time, nor the irregular way in which the sequences of its telling alternated between abbreviation and elaboration, between topicalizing
and generalizing, between Poles and Irishmen.
But more importantly for the present argument,
the truth is that with joke-telling as with most
folk-arts, what shows up in the museum is not a
typical representative, but a special case that
does not look altogether like the run of the
mill. The story well-told is not the evolution-
ary product of a logical succession of stages
of growth, the triumph of orderly laws; it is
rather, in most cases, a creative rescue operation, effected despite the botched and awkward
versions of the joke already in circulation. If
all that gets saved for posterity are the museum
pieces, who will guess how wildly irregular were
the other versions of the same tale, how randomly changes were introduced as it passed from
person to person, how greatly the clumsy joke-
tellers outnumbered the memorably talented ones?

I appeal to your experience. Of the last
dozen stories you have heard, probably only one
or two were really distinguished, and three or
four might better have remained unspoken. The

majority of participants, on whose behavior the
character of the form-history especially depends,
tend to deform the stories in a rich and unpredictable variety of ways. When their tellers
try to reconstruct them from their experienced
but imperfect memories, and even when they attempt to insert creative improvements, they often forget or distort crucial information, import irrelevant motifs or formulas from the general tradition, bungle important lines of development and make careless substitutions for particular elements of the original version. When
they do so, they may or may not be aware of
something wrong; most likely, they will realize
only that their auditors are not quite as amused
as they themselves had been at first hearing.
That is, if they had originally heard their
stories well told; for it is also statistically
probable that they too had heard them in equally, though perhaps differently, mangled versions.

Let me illustrate by offering examples of
four ways in which joke-telling typically breaks
down. Each of these examples is historical, not
factitious, and each is representative of an important mode of clumsiness with direct relevance
to corresponding features of gospel pericopes
and their transmission.

The first example is an illustration of
Informational Improvidence. The relevance of a

particular story to a given situation may be
apparent to the sharp-eyed even when no direct
connections are made, and under conditions of
political censorship or social discretion, stories have successfully circulated as effectual
parables, understood as applying to persons or
events to which they innocently withhold any
explicit reference. But under normal conditions, wittiness need not be so tactful, and
the creative teller introduces a new cast of
characters to make an old story topical, or re-
designs the setting in order to introduce a
closer relevance to the experience or concerns
of his audience. Some stories are highly port-
able, and can be redecorated or restaffed to
suit a wide variety of occasions. Most ethnic
jokes can be shifted about and applied directly,
without significant loss, to whatever local pop-
ulation is currently being thus abused—and, of
course, many of them had an earlier ethnically
unspecified existence as moron jokes. But a
few of these have twists in them that apply not
to any silly person but to real or fancied characteristics of a specific group, or to the peculiarities of a particular historical situation. In these cases, success depends upon
providing, pointedly enough, the contextual information upon which the thrust of the story
depends. Failure to provide may change the

character, effect, and even intelligibility of
the tale. A story currently in circulation concerns a man who walks into a pub in Northern
Ireland, carrying under his arm a crocodile
painted bright green, and inquires in a firm
and aggressive voice, "Do you serve Protestants
here?" "We do," replies the publican. "Then,"
says the customer, "I'll have a Guinness for me-
self, and a Protestant for me crocodile." I recently heard this repeated by a university history instructor, to whom I had told it not long
before in essentially the form given above. The
teller—a Protestant, incidentally—started out
thus: "A man walked into a bar with an alligator
under his arm and asked the bartender if he
served Protestants. The bartender said, 'Yes,
we serve anybody.'..." Deprived of its canoni-
cal setting, the story loses the contextualiza-
tion that makes it marginally worth telling,
and at the same time subtly shifts its focus
from the original caricature of a topically
poignant type of Irish Catholic bigotry to an
unmotivated and abstracted anti-Protestantism.
Mere informational improvidence has made it impossible to deduce from this form of the story
the setting in social and political history that
originally gave it point; anyone attempting to
make rigorous inferences from the revised version would very likely totally misunderstand

the disposition of the teller and the background
out of which the tale was begotten.

It is one thing to fail to provide necessary information; it is another to provide it
inaccurately and misleadingly. My second example of deformation is of this type, Inadvertent
Dislocation. Many elements of many stories are
highly adjustable, and the story will work
equally well if something in the same category
is substituted for the item originally used. It
may be set indifferently in Pittsburgh or Louis-
ville, perhaps even in Dijon or Osaka; the protagonist may be male or female, of any nation-
ality, betting on any team in any sport. But
what seems superficially like a satisfactorily
near equivalent to the original will not always
do. In the present instance, the teller took
care to provide the informational background on
which the story depends, but unreflectively
substituted a close alternative for one of the
original elements. It was more interesting in
that the person in question, a member of the
Board of Education of the city of Toronto, had
told the tale successfully at least once before
in my presence, at which time it was presented
as a purportedly real-life story of a sidewalk
radio interviewer in World War II America who
approached a WAVE and asked her to tell the
radio audience about her branch of the service,

adding that "Looking at your uniform, I can see
you're naval." The pun-value of the final
words, however, was definitively obscured on
this later occasion when the teller began the
story by identifying the woman as a WAC. The
resulting effect is still slightly racy, especially as a real radio interview: some listener
may subsequently have supposed that to be the
point, and passed the WAC version on unchanged.

In this last case, the punch-line of the
story was accurately remembered, but was dissi-
pated by the inadvertent dislocation of an element on which its effect crucially depended.
Often, it is the other way around: for many
punchlines are carefully and precisely crafted
into an irreformable formula of words, and may
lose most or all of their effectiveness if uncertain or careless or inattentive memory repro-
duces them with even the slightest change. The
problem of Formal Breakdown, with which my next
example is concerned, can affect a story in
other ways as well. I recently heard a fairly
amusing joke somewhat diminished when its original three-stage climax, carefully arranged to
produce a crescendo, was adjusted by a professor
of philosophy, who transposed the last two
stages; and since then have heard the same joke
considerably diminished by a doctoral candidate
who omitted the first two stages altogether.

Tinkering with significant form will readily
impoverish a story, and tinkering with the
punch-line (often the most rigorously uncompro-
misable aspect of formal order in the story,
and the absolute condition of its success) may
simply bankrupt it. For instance: my grandmother once reported to me that in her younger
and more frivolous days, she told a joke to a
companion on the way to a party. "Can a cow
drink beer?" she inquired. Her companion con-
fessed that she didn't know. "Not a whole
stein," returned my witty grandmother, confident that no one in that rural community could
possibly be ignorant that Holstein cattle were
the commonest local breed. Her companion was
richly amused——so much so that she asked and
secured my grandmother's permission to put the
question to the rest of the party. She subsequently did so. "Can a cow drink beer?" she
asked, with suppressed anticipatory chuckles.
No one knew. "A Holstein can't," **sai**d she, dis-
solving with unearned laughter. The rest of
the guests probably joined in, feeling uneasily
obtuse but not necessarily unwilling to try it
out on friends.

A fourth type of breakdown is one that
derives not from omission or mismanagement of
information, nor from distortion of indispensable formal structures (large or small) but

from a global failure of the teller to grasp
the main import of the tale: Massive Misunderstanding. An intelligent lady of my acquaint-
ance once retold a story which contained a touch
of interest that had caught her fancy enough to
motivate her to pass it on. But her point of
interest was not the point of the story. I do
not know what version she had heard, but the
one she told, though bent to the angle of her
interest, contained fossils of an earlier version. Here and there were clues recognizable
to those whose lives have passed through locker
rooms, clues betraying that this was once essentially a bawdy joke whose real original drift
she had innocently failed to perceive. I ask
you to take my word for it, and to leave the
matter diplomatically imprecise; but I acknowledge the right to evidence and example, and
should such a gingerly reporting be insufficient
to persuade critical readers of the possibility
of this kind of clumsiness and misunderstanding
within experienced circles, I respectfully refer
them to another instance, identical in kind,
which has been contributed to the tradition by
the former President of the United States: it
may be found straddling columns two and three
in a publication recounting "some of President
Ford's favorite jokes, exactly as he tells them"[3]
—where you may also find alternative examples

of this and other types of anecdotal abuses, in
a brief but brilliantly sustained display of
versatile deformation in what might formerly
have seemed to be virtually foolproof stories.

The examples above are not drawn from
the works of the egregiously obtuse. All the
principals were intelligent persons, rather well
educated, and with some sophisticated experience of the world. Their unsuccess in these
instances was simply a function of their not
being unusually gifted and disciplined story-
tellers, which left them vulnerable to typical
missteps which only the most skillful consistently avoid. Ordinariness in the setting-forth
of stories is quite sufficient for the achievement of striking blunders and even total disasters. There is no need for exceptional inep-
titude.

I have concentrated on instances of dramatic massive breakdown, but the reader will
have noted that the major examples were supplemented by less spectacular instances of clumsiness that did not obliterate the stories entirely but reduced and diffused their effectiveness.
Examples of this lesser mismanagement can be
multiplied indefinitely: a college president
who weakened the thrust of a joke by using the
standard device of having the protagonist try
the same thing twice without result and then

make a third attempt that precipitates the crucial reaction, even though the story (at least
as he told it) was quite unsuited to that mode
of development; and a lawyer who forgot some
important considerations at the beginning of
the tale and barely remembered to stuff them in
parenthetically at the last moment, just before
the punch-line; and many others who counterpro-
ductively abbreviated or expanded, wandered in
their attention and focus, created dysfunction-
al ambiguities, confused characters, omitted
important connections, displaced critical em-
phases. (I once had the pleasure of seeing
Vaughan Monroe forget the words at the turning
point of "Blue Moon," and smoothly supply alternatives that utterly reversed the main dramatic event of the song.) General defectiveness
is the rule, not the exception, and the teller
who merely disadvantages a story most of the
time may at any moment completely ruin one by a
standard error or lapse of memory or misplaced
creative gesture.

My examples have concentrated mainly on
instances in which I happen to be in a position
to know the version of the story that had come
to the teller in question, and therefore can
pinpoint the agent, and describe the nature, of
the existential blunder. But I remind you that
this is possibly only in unusual circumstances,

and does not represent the normal character of this oral tradition. When one hears a joke that comes off with poor or mediocre results, it is not fair to blame the immediate teller: he may be passing on with exact fidelity the version told to him. That earlier version may in turn be true to its predecessor. Perhaps it was three or four stages back that some link in the chain introduced the disappointing distortion that none of the succeeding tellers thought, or knew how, to correct. Ten stages earlier may have occurred a different sort of mishandling, whose influence may leave a curious residue in the tradition without showing itself clearly enough to be discerned, reconstructed, and corrected. The overall process cannot be rigorously described. Every once in a while, one may come upon a decidedly superior version of a story one had heard told in essentially similar weakened forms on several previous occasions— but how is one to know if this welcome version is *fons et origo* itself, miraculously preserved in its integrity despite the perils of oral tradition, or an inventive and appropriate improvement, just recently hatched from the brain of a creative contributor who saw what might be done for the tired tale she had received? You could ask the teller, of course; but he is likely to reply that he is just telling it the way he

heard it, and that it's really X's joke——while
X, if sought out, will credit it to Y, his immediate predecessor. Y will only remember that
he heard it at a convention, and can't recall
from whom. The flow of tradition, traced back,
disappears into the sands of time. In the present, it continues to ebb and eddy in various
unpredictable ways. The development is fortu-
nately not governed by Gresham's Law——but neither does it follow Darwin's.

II. FORM CRITICISM

"The proper understanding of form-criti-
cism," wrote Bultmann, "rests upon the judgment
that the literature in which the life of a given
community, even the primitive Christian community, has taken shape, springs out of quite definite conditions and wants of life from which
grows up a quite definite style and quite specific forms and categories."[4] Thus the twin pillars on which form criticism was founded, a
claim about the definiteness of the conditioning motives and a complementary claim about the
corresponding definiteness and regularity of
the conditioned results. The judgment which
Bultmann thought one must make in order to understand properly is still being made. Harald
Riesenfeld, for instance, recently observed

that through form criticism, "we now know, for
instance, that a parable or an account of a miracle took shape in accordance with definite
stylistic laws which can be seen at work in
transformations of all items of the same kind."[5]
How definite are these laws? How rigorously is
this process determined? Very definite and very
rigorously, it appears. Bultmann's language—
"springs out of, grows up"—may sound both open
and organic, but Riesenfeld's sense of the matter is more accurately deterministic. Bultmann
wrote of "the laws governing the formulation of
popular narrative and tradition," confidently
asserting that these laws "may be studied in detail in the material which the Synoptists hand
down."[6] Definite conditions, definite results:
twin pillars.

Form criticism had, of course, to specify
the definite wants of life that obtained in earliest Christian days. The specification that has
been most pervasively dominant in form-critical
work is probably the one that, in a most dramatic and revolutionary way, ushered in a whole new
era in Gospel criticism and buried an earlier
one: it is the kerygmatic need. Casting aside
the labors of previous generations, the pioneers
of form criticism boldly denied that the Gospels
offer much in the way of accurate history or biography, and claimed that it did not much matter:

the Gospels are not recording but proclaiming,
and the proclamation is of the risen Lord, not
of the carpenter of Nazareth. Starting largely
as an assumption, this supposition appeared to
be confirmed in the course of its application
as a principle of form criticism, so much so
that it is now commonly assumed in scholarly
circles that form criticism has established (to
quote Conzelmann) "that the Gospels are in
their nature and purpose not a historical record or a biography of Jesus: their purpose is
the proclamation of saving events."[7] That
statement is worth a closer look.

The first part of Conzelmann's statement
represents a valuable correction of earlier presuppositions about the Gospels which credited
them with strong historical purpose and relia-
bility, and keen biographical interests. Such
assumptions are, if not demonstrably false, at
least fatally inadequate. The Gospels simply
do not behave in those ways; close attention
shows that neither their content nor their manner can be claimed to support the traditional
naive supposition. Careful discernment of the
overall ways in which their individual stories
developed and changed clearly shows that something else was at work, something else at stake.
Form criticism has made this mark, probably as
a permanent achievement from which scholarship

will never turn back.

But the first part of Conzelmann's statement, if helpfully corrective, is too implausi-
bly flat in its denial. The Gospels are not
essentially a historical record, but who, reading the opening verses of the Gospel of Luke,
can avoid conceding that their author had the
achievement of an accurate historical record
among his important purposes? The Gospels are
not biographies in the sense that has been ac-
quired for that term by practitioners of the
sophisticated modern genre of biography, but it
is perfectly obvious that they mean to represent to us (as Luke puts it) "what Jesus did
and taught," which can hardly be called an un-
biographical aim. As with the Gospels in general, so with many of the individual pericopes
of which they are composed: even before their
collection into running accounts of the doings
and teachings of Jesus, they manifest an interest in the historical record and in the life-
work of their central subject. Historical record and biography cannot be simply excluded
from a description of their nature and purpose,
even if they may not be allowed to define them.

The second part of Conzelmann's statement shows the pendulum at the apogee of its
alternative swing: "their purpose is the proclamation of saving events." Conzelmann claims

that this has been established under the *aegis*
of form criticism. The claim is highly misleading, the more so in that it purports to be
the result of a rigorous critical process.
What Conzelmann puts forward is not an inexorable deduction, but a tenuous inference, no
less tenuous or inferential for its having been
adopted by the vast majority of scholars who
endorse the results of form-critical methods.
It has not been *established,* but only *asserted*
and *accepted;* and critically, there is a world
of difference between the two. The Gospels are
clearly concerned with saving events; but to
characterize them exclusively as proclamation
of saving events is an important begging of the
question. The Gospels are full of stories. All
these stories relate to Jesus, and each has
some point of significance that qualifies it
for inclusion in a general overview of "what
Jesus did and taught." But to suppose that a
report of what Jesus did and taught is necessarily a proclamation, or that all of the Gospel reports may appropriately be described as
versions of "saving events," is far from obvious, especially when one ponders such disparate
items as Herod's fateful promise to Salome, the
cursing of the fig tree, the prediction and realization of Peter's denial. The Gospels are
gatherings of significant stories about Jesus

(and others connected with him). To claim as
much more than this as Conzelmann claims, is to
project into them thoroughgoing Evangelistic
principles that we have no compelling reason to
believe were consistently the program of those
whom we retrospectively, and with tendentious
overtones, call Evangelists.

If one accepts the proposition that the
early Synoptic traditions were reliably determined in a definite and specific way by the
conditions and wants of life that obtained, and
supposes that early Christians had a relentless
singlemindedness about the one project of proclaiming Jesus Christ, then the foundations of
form criticism appear unshakeably firm. But
why should such assumptions be made? Why should
anyone follow Bultmann into the impossibly ex-
treme claim that "the interest of the gospels
is absolutely different from that of the modern
historian,"[8] when the Gospels do not behave as
if they are governed by a single interest or
are absolutely uninterested in what concerns
modern historians? And why on the other hand
presume that the Gospels "were meant to be read
as proclamations"[9] when there are no adequate
indications that their purposes are unitary and
consistent, let alone identifiable in this specific way, and when we simply do not know how
they were meant to be read?

The achievements of form criticism are
considerable, and some of them are probably
permanent; but the hand has been overplayed.
The assumption that we can know only indirectly
and artificially what an oral tradition is like
is, in the face of contemporary joke-telling,
significantly false. The assumption that the
Gospels' stories lend themselves to the deduction of formal and rigorous rules governing the
various types of story, permitting reliable inferences about the contexts, motives, develop-
mental directions, historical trajectory, and
the like, is an assumption that can be sustained only if we accept the fiction that the
process of oral transmission is unfamiliar and
must be artificially reconstructed. Methodolo-
gically attractive as it may be to suppose that
there are specific "characteristics of primitive story telling"[10] that left the stories in-
variably determined by conditioning circumstances in collusion with narrative laws to
which the stories were uniformly obedient, I
suggest that such a supposition collapses with
implausibility in the presence of the modern
tradition of joke-telling. The process could
not possibly have been as rigorously deterministic nor as economically simple as form critics have presumed.

No, I suggest that it makes far more

sense to begin with quite a different sort of
assumption, being more faithful to plausibility
and evidence on the one hand, and on the other,
learning from the character of the one oral
tradition that can counsel us most immediately.
The Gospels emerge from various specific conditions and various wants of life that exerted a
varying influence on shaping the materials
formed and passed down in early Christian circles.   Proclamation was one of the motives at
work; but it competed with a measure of plain
curiosity about what Jesus had done and said,
a taste for engaging and entertaining stories,
and many other considerations that must inevitably prevent our being able to reconstruct the
development of tradition along clean lines.
Furthermore, in addition to being formed according to a much more complex and unpredictable set of considerations, these stories passed
through a variety of tellers who varied in
their motives, their competence, their creativity; and when they changed the stories they
told, which they inevitably did, through mis-
memory or blunder or deliberate adjustment,
they introduced another set of variables.

        In short, if we take a more realistic
view of the matter, we can readily get the impression that the form-critical project is not
nearly so well founded as is often supposed,

the results not nearly so reliable and sound.
The perennial truths of story-telling flow in a
different fashion, with more complex and unpredictable eddies, and the character of the process does not permit the kind of inferences we
would like to be able to make. I submit that
the enduring oral tradition of joke-telling provides a fruitful analogue to the process by
which the Synoptic gospel-tradition was preserved and developed, and that we should accordingly approach the history of Gospel forms with
the realization that we receive them from a succession of largely ordinary (and therefore somewhat awkward if randomly creative) story-tellers
who told tales, more or less significant, about
Jesus, and that we can neither hope to pin down
consistently just what the history was, nor
understand its products adequately, without
making room for the special critical uncertainty
principle of clumsiness.

III.   REDACTION CRITICISM

"Thirty years ago," wrote Henry Hogarth
in 1972, "it was commonly held that the writer
of Mark's Gospel was a simple countryman who
collected stories and strung them together in a
rough chronicle. The emergency of redaction
criticism has changed all this."[11] The calendar

is approximately right. The early triumph of
form criticism distracted the attention of
scholars to the individual units of the Gospels,
at the expense of the gathered character of the
collections themselves. But the very differences among the received Gospels made it impossible that this imbalance could be sustained
for very long. Within the last generation, vig-
orous attention has been given to them individ-
ually, to examine what each evangelist actually
did with the materials he inherited from the
history of developing pre-gospel forms. Creativity was once more allowed to enter the picture. The presuppositions of form criticism
were mainly left curiously undisturbed: the materials that fell to the hands of the gospel
writers were still normally regarded as defined
by laws of development, their sequence of oral
transmitters implicitly characterized as unin-
ventive functions of the pressures of circum-
stance and the rules governing individual forms.
But the evangelists themselves became recognized
as capable of inflecting specific stories in a
purposeful way, selecting from the available
store and editorializing in introductions and
summaries in accordance with theological pro-
grams of their own. Redaction criticism was
born.

Critics have long since rejected the view

that Mark was "a mere colorless compiler of impersonal anecdotes."[12]   The emergence of redaction criticism has indeed changed all this.
The change has been effected, however, in a
curiously unreflective way. If form criticism
tended, and still tends, to exaggerate the determinism of impersonal laws, redaction criticism has tended from its inception to exaggerate the masterful control with which the evangelist orchestrated his received material to
the tune of his special ideas and purposes.
Now we are offered a Gospel of Mark that is to
be thought of as "the studied product of genius"
which can "on every page...reveal the definite,
deliberate, and conscious craftsmanship of the
author."[13]   In the history of criticism, a
great shift of the aeons seems to have taken
place between the pre-Gospel history of determined forms and the emergence of the theologically creative redactors of Gospels.

     It was time that a margin of human versa-
tility be allowed a place in the action. But
once again, an important principle has been
neglected. The determinism of form criticism
made too little allowance for individual and
random clumsiness; the respect for evangelist
artistry accorded by the standard suppositions
of redaction criticism makes the same mistake.
I suggest that the analogy by which I have

questioned form criticism may be usefully extended into redaction criticism as well.

Admittedly, the extension is not auto-
matic. I acknowledge a vast difference between
a joke told and a joke written. It is a difference that makes itself felt with particular
poignancy whenever one hears a story told precisely in the manner in which it had appeared
somewhere in print (the literary recasting
sounds stilted when uttered aloud) or when one,
reading a transcript of oral proceedings, finds
a story reproduced there *verbatim* (even the
most successfully amusing performance may find
itself reduced to a pitifully flat and thin
ghost of what it had been). The more successful literary recorders of jokes make use of a
repertoire of distinctly noncolloquial vocabu-
lary, sentence-structure, and types of conden-
sations to compensate for the loss of the leav-
en of timing, accent, emphasis, expression.
The better the written rendition, the more it
departs from the spoken one.

But the more successful writers of jokes
are, like the more successful *raconteurs,* exceptional. Indeed, they may be expected—even
in a highly literate society—to be still rarer
than their oral counterparts, since theirs is
the demanding office of capturing a story live
in its native habitat and translating it to a

quite different climate in which it will reproduce only with considerable coddling. It is a
sophisticated calling. And if it is attempted
by someone who lacks the requisite sophistica-
tion, who either does not adequately appreciate
how different the two media **are** or lacks technical expertise in literary matters, the obvious
result is the application in writing of the
same sub-literary techniques with which the oral
medium is managed. That is: in very ordinary
circumstances, the phenomenology of the oral
tradition will carry over extensively into the
process of redaction. The pathologies will remain largely the same in the individual unit.
In extended sequences, they are likely to be
firmly analogous.

        The literary redactors of the Gospel tra-
ditions are likely *a priori,* in fact, to be
among the relatively undistinguished members of
the oral tradition, and therefore to manifest
various of the breakdowns that occur there. For
(to revert one last time to the world of the
analogy) although in lucky and affluent times,
one may be graced in published joke-collections
with the efforts of an Isaac Asimov, or at least
a Bennett Cerf, that is a rare good fortune.
History has not always been so kind. Nor should
it be expected to be: for the really skillful
practitioner of joke-telling will rarely write

his stories down. He is too keenly aware of
what they must lose in the translation, no matter how careful he may be to preserve their max-
imum integrity in their literary confinement.
For that reason alone it would be probable that
most of the compilations of printed jests, from
Eulenspiegel and the *Hundred Merry Tales* to the
anonymous collections marketed for unwary modern
toastmasters, have been perpetrated by the less
skillful, frequently working from already dis-
torted oral traditions which they were not in a
position to set right, and adding further dis-
tortions of their own in bursts of misguided
creativity. One has only to read some of these
collections to demonstrate that a want of skill
is a standard condition among the authors: and
some are downright clumsy. And so it is likely
to be with the first collections of Gospel materials.

These collections are not, however, *mere*
collections. I acknowledge the rightness of the
redaction-critical recognition that the role of
the evangelist is not exhausted in his editorial
tinkering with individual pericopes. There are
matters of selection, of arrangement, of interpretive introduction and summary, that must inevitably have gone into the composition of Gospels. In any of these ways too the redactor
was at some degree of liberty to introduce his

prepossessions—and his clumsiness. He shared
with the creative tradition that went before
him the capacity to organize themes, motifs,
theories, explanations. He also shared with
that tradition the capacity to misunderstand,
to be inconsistent, to attempt creative contributions that could go astray.

The remainder of this book is dedicated
to the proposition that the Gospel of Mark
shows evidence of just such a distorting clumsiness as besets the ordinary, if occasionally
creative talented, story-teller in every time
and place. If I am correct in thinking that we
should change the usual assumptions in the ways
for which I have argued, then it will not be
easy to separate the peculiar contribution of
Marcan clumsiness from the random deformations
that had occurred before him. After all, he
may have preserved with puzzled misgivings certain oddities in his received material with
which he did not suppose he had a right to tam-
per. I do not attempt to make, because I do
not believe that we are in a position to make,
rigorous distinctions between what Mark received
and what he gave forth. I have certain suspi-
cions about which is which, and will argue them
in due place: but the dominant point is the uni-
versal applicability of the principle of clumsi-

ness. It matters little whether in a given instance it is really to be charged up to Mark or
to his predecessors. What counts is the contention that it is in fact operating. I am therefore not impugning the intelligence of Mark or
of those who went before him. I consider it a
serious procedural error to suppose that the
presence of clumsiness indicates a lack of intelligence, just as I think it a serious procedural error to suppose that the presence of
intelligence necessarily implies a consistently
controlled purposeful command over one's material. Or even over one's creativity. I mean to
suggest that the contemporary search for subtle
innuendo in Marcan pericopes (on the basis of
the laws of form criticism) and the parallel
search for subtle innuendo in Marcan editorial
touches (on the basis of the programmatic assumptions of redaction criticism) are importantly misguided attempts to project finesse into
the awkward performances of ordinarily weak, if
occasionally talented and creative, story-tellers of ancient times——and that we can make better sense of some important Marcan problems if
we approach them accordingly. My argument will
consist of a survey of Mark's first chapter and
a commentary on three selected pericopes from
elsewhere in his Gospel. I will then apply it
to an examination of one important and proble-

matic theme which has long troubled the readers
of Mark: the Esoteric Teaching.

CHAPTER TWO

MARK'S OPENING PAGES

The exercise called "close reading" is an art, not a science. There are various ways of going about it and they produce equally various results. A great deal depends upon the frame of expectations which the reader brings to the occasion. Careful reviewers look to the text for guidance to see what sort of audience is envisioned, what sort of performance is intended, so as to avoid the common error of blaming an appropriately solemn utterance for being stuffy, or a playful one for being frivolous, merely because the reader had arbitrarily expected a different tone. It is inappropriate to evaluate fledgling essays on How I Spent My Summer Vacation according to the standards set by the likes of Sir Thomas Browne and E. B. White, or to weigh legal documents in the stylistic balance of tabloid journalism. Much cheap fun has been had from doing so, both

spitefully and playfully. You have probably encountered several such parodies in print: the
Gettysburg Address treated as a highschool essay
("'Fourscore and seven years ago?! Pretentious.
Say 87"), or "Diddle Diddle Dumpling" explicated
as if it were a deeply symbolic poem. None of
us is safe from such blunders in reading; we all
can remember (though we would rather not) certain embarrassing episodes arising from this
form of clumsiness. I dutifully acknowledge
that I may be about to perpetrate yet another.

To read a passage clumsily is one sort of
fault. To read a passage's clumsinesses as if
they were graceful is another. If one is to
choose prudently between potential faults on the
basis of social success, it is obvious which way
to go: the traditions of snobbery make it inevitable that you will eventually be hooted out
of the room if you sneer, in the presence of the
defensively cultured, at what seem to you curiously bad moments in the poetry of T. S. Eliot
or Ezra Pound (boorish!), while the same audience is likely on the whole to offer reverent
attention if you should claim to find deep
resonances in "The Lullaby of Broadway" or the
slapdash ballad on "Finnegan's Wake." The
standards are unpredictable: it is fashionable
to scoff at Kilmer's "Trees" for its imagistic

incoherence, and equally fashionable to cele-
brate Donne's "A Valediction: of my Name in the
Window" for its daring versatility—though I
have yet to hear an articulate explanation of
why the epithet applied to the one poem might
not equally be applied to the other.

It is fashionable to treat the Gospel of
Mark solemnly, respectfully, as if it were a
carefully crafted piece of writing with deep
purposes in view. It is distinctly gauche to
grumble about its style (which is sometimes
thought to be elegantly economical, and at
worst normally considered honest and simple) or
its organization (which is thought to be subtly
rich).[14] I intend in the following pages to be
that sort of distinctly gauche. I think Mark
writes rather badly. I wish to show how and
why I think so by subjecting his first chapter
to a "close reading"—not unmindful of the
dangerous presumptions involved—that will be
saturated with my conviction (which I think I
have earned) that he is a clumsy author. The
ultimate test is, of course, whether my remarks
ring true. I claim no authority that is not
shared with you. Judge.

I.   INDIVIDUAL UNITS

Note: The translations that follow are

based on the current Nestle and Aland editions
of the Greek New Testament, with occasional
side-glances at Vincent Taylor's edition of
Mark. I have attempted to render the texts
literally enough to reproduce some of the fla-
vors and awkwardnesses of the Greek that are
normally muted and smoothed out in modern translations, and idiomatically enough not to give
an exaggerated impression of them. Rather than
burden the passages, and the reader, with the
extensive annotations necessary to explain the
grounds for alternative readings or the justi-
fications for choice of words or the apparent
deviations from standard translations, I will
simply register the fact that I have tried to
be careful, accurate, and fair, and believe
that questions about whether I have succeeded
can be resolved, mainly in my favor, by re-
course to standard commentaries and reference-
books—though of course the experienced reader
will readily realize that there are various
complications in the textual witnesses, the vo-
cabulary, the possibilities of punctuation, and
the nuances of grammar that will leave even
careful judgments provisional, precarious, and
moot.

> A. 1:1-6 The beginning of the good
> news of Jesus Christ [Son of God].
> As it stands written in Isaiah

the prophet, "Behold, I send
my messenger before your face,
who will prepare your way. A
voice crying in the wilderness,
'Prepare the way of the Lord,
make straight his paths.'"
There was John baptizing in
the wilderness, [and] proclaiming a baptism of repentance
for the forgiveness of sins.
And all the country of Judea
went out to him, and all the
Jerusalemites; and they were
baptized in the Jordan river
by him, confessing their sins.
Now, John was wearing camel
hair, and a leather belt
around his loins, and eating
locusts and wild honey.

Mark evidently inherited the application of
Isaiah's Voice Crying in the Wilderness (itself
being a clumsy mistranslation of the Hebrew
original, which has an unlocated voice crying
about what is to happen in the wilderness) from
the general tradition: Matthew and Luke share
the quotation, Luke expanding it from the subsequent verses of Isaiah. Mark alone adds the
quotation—conflated from Exodus 23:20 and
Malachi 3:1—about the Messenger, but he omits
to credit his source, leaving the impression
that the entire passage comes from Isaiah.
Awkward. When it comes to the description of
John's apparel and diet, Matthew provides a
good comparison for the standards of discretion.

Matthew gives these details as part of the introductory scene-setting, without calling particular attention to them. Mark places them in
such a manner as to give them independent emphasis. It appears to be an afterthought detail. At any rate, it is pointlessly anticlimactic and distracting for it to be slipped in
between the two pieces of much more important
information, and especially when it is introduced in this misleadingly emphatic new-para-
graph manner with the repetition of John's name.
Or should we take the signals otherwise, and
presume that this is intended to be a highly
significant remark, worthy of such emphasis?
If so, we are left helpless to divine its significance. One rescuing strategy is to credit
Mark with a subtle and telling allusion to the
resemblance between John and Elijah. This will
not do, for two reasons. In the first place,
subtle allusion is not in keeping with the
style he has already established: he has already given special emphasis to the detail of
the wilderness setting[15] (separating it from
the accompanying details in a way that Matthew
and Luke do not), apparently in order to drive
home a correspondence with a text which he
takes the trouble to quote. The strategy is
entirely overt. Why would he withhold such

demonstrations of his meaning in a case that is
far less obvious? It is as easy to mention
Elijah as Isaiah, and as easy to quote supporting texts in one instance as another. And in
the second place, if this is meant as an allusion to Elijah, it is very badly handled. The
details given are not clearly reminiscent of
any scriptural text or any known Targum. The
mention of locusts, for instance, would be pur-
poseless and distracting in such an allusional
attempt (there is no known association of Elijah
with locusts), and would thus be needlessly sub-
versive to any putative alignment of John with
Elijah.[16] One way or another, one must conclude
that this is not controlled purposefulness but
random and disordered detail.

> B.   1:7-8 And John proclaimed,
>   saying: "The one more power-
>   ful than I comes after [me],
>   the strap of whose sandals
>   I am not worthy, stooping
>   down, to untie. I baptize[d]
>   you in water; but he will
>   baptize you in holy spirit."

Matthew and Luke first give us the authoritative
preaching of John and then have him mention the
one coming after him, "the more powerful than
I" (*ho ischeroteros mou*). The ordering is intelligible. Mark offers no introductory preaching by John and thus leaves him a disappointing

anticlimax, after all his buildup, when he
finally opens his mouth to proclaim that the
one more powerful than he (what power has
been established for *him*?) is coming after.
Matthew and Luke, by first mentioning "the
one who comes after me" (possibly a technical
general title, "The One Who Comes After Me),
make the definite article in "the one more
powerful than I" fall generally into place.
Mark's abrupt mention of "the one more powerful than I," without antecedent, leaves the
definite article seeming doubly odd. By con-
sulting Matthew and Luke, we know what he
means and have a sense of what materials he
must have been working with. In that context,
we can understand him. But we are forced to
conclude that his treatment of this part of
his story arises from an insensitive and im-
provident truncation of the fuller and more
intelligible version of the same materials
that can be found satisfactorily rendered in
Matthew and Luke.

> C. 1:9-11 And it came to pass in
> those days that Jesus from
> Nazareth of Galilee came, and
> was baptized in the Jordan by
> John. And forthwith coming up
> out of the water, he saw the
> heavens splitting, and the
> spirit as a dove descending

> upon him. And a voice out
> of the heavens, "You are my
> son, the beloved one, in you
> I delight."

This passage seems to me rather well handled,
apart from the rather pointlessly emphatic
"forthwith (or "suddenly," "immediately":
euthus). I suspect, however, that if we were
not so used to settling for the text as it
stands, we would feel slightly ill-served in
being given no information about how Jesus or
the others who are present reacted to such re-
markable happenings. I do not think that dramatic economy is the answer: that is not a policy consistently pursued by Mark even thus far.
Much is evidently expected to be taken for
granted; that is surely legitimate, but its
management here (or lack of management) is hardly to the credit of the author.

> D.   1:12-13 And forthwith the
>   spirit drives him out into
>   the wilderness. And he was
>   in the wilderness forty days,
>   being tempted by the accuser
>   [*tou satana*], and was with
>   the wild beasts, and the angels
>   ministered [were ministering]
>   to him.

This terse reference to the Temptation would offer us little of intelligible significance were
it not for the happy chance that we know a

fuller story from Matthew and Luke. Surely
this must be a condensation of some such longer
and more pointedly meaningful account of the
event—a condensation that is both arbitrary
and unskillful. We are used to thinking that
the angels ministered once the temptation was
concluded, but that is from Matthew and Luke:
Mark gives us only an aimless conjunction that
does not establish a separation between these
parts of the experience: in fact, it encourages
the impression that they were simultaneous,
which dulls the potentially dramatic effect of
the temptation itself, by comparison with the
alternative and fuller versions of the story.
Admittedly, Matthew and Luke may be "improving"
the original, which may (like Mark, less dramatically) have allowed Jesus to be solaced by
angels in the course of the temptations. Mark
is therefore not necessarily to be faulted in
this instance. But no one can deny that the
vague and ineffectual remark that Jesus in this
episode was "with the wild beasts" is unsatisfactory, poised between saying too little and
saying too much. Commentators have inevitably
suggested that this is an abbreviation of a
lost episode that once had a point. Be that as
it may, the postulated point is lost along with
the putative fuller version.[17] Mark's abbrevi-

ation is impossibly mild and vague, as if he believes that this detail is significant but does
not know—or at least does not quite tell—how.

> E. 1:14-15 Now, after the de-
>   livering up of John, Jesus
>   came into Galilee, proclaim-
>   ing the good news of God [and
>   saying] that "The season has
>   been completed, and the do-
>   minion of God is at hand:
>   repent, and have faith in the
>   good news."

This account of the beginnings of Jesus' public
ministry has strong effect. It may be worth
noting, however, that Mark here abandons the
tidy (if artificial) space- and time-linkages
that he has provided up to this point.[18] Jesus
was in the desert, and John presumably went on
baptizing. Suddenly John is already arrested
(when and why did this take place?)[19] and Jesus
comes into Galilee (whence? from the desert?
and why does Mark use such a neutral word as
came [*ēlthen*] when he has already troubled to
emphasize that Galilee was the starting point
of Jesus' public career? one would expect something like *returned*, if Mark is to be consistently purposeful).[20] It is obviously reasonable to wonder whether there is any meaningful
connection between the two events of John's imprisonment and the beginning of Jesus' career

of preaching. Other Gospels seem to try to
deal with this question. Mark simply juxta-
poses them, and neither tells nor implies any
relationship other than temporal sequence. He
does not relate John's imprisonment to his previous account of John, nor does he relate the
beginning of Jesus' public ministry to his previous account of Jesus. It appears as though
Mark is content to recall that these details
and sequences were mentioned in the version
that came to him, and will settle for passing
them on, for whatever they are worth, without
troubling to coordinate them with anything that
has gone before, geographically, temporally, or
thematically. I am disinclined to suppose that
the missing of the opportunities is dramatically purposeful. What purpose?

> F. 1:16-20 And passing along by
> the Sea of Galilee, he saw
> Simon and Andrew the brother
> of Simon casting a net in the
> sea; for they were fishermen.
> And Jesus said to them, "Come
> follow me, and I will make you
> to be fishers of men." And
> forthwith leaving their nets,
> they followed him. And going
> on a little farther, he saw
> James the [son] of Zebedee and
> John his brother, and they in
> the ship mending the nets. And
> forthwith he called them; and

>   leaving their father Zebedee
>   in the ship with the hired
>   servants, they went after
>   him.

Forthwith [*euthus*] has already become a Marcan
mannerism. The first instance in this passage
is dramatically effective; but the second is
oddly placed and without evident function. Presumably, the original intent in the latter instance was to emphasize once again the prompt
response of the disciples to the summons, but
the way Mark puts it merely makes the summons
itself prompt, not the reaction. It seems evident that the key word was displaced from its
intended slot through clumsiness. In my judgment, to tell your reader that these men were
casting a fishing net into the sea, and *then* to
add the observation that they were fishermen,
is scarcely to give evidence of tactful artistry. To say, without excuse or apology, that
they left their father and the hired help to
their own resources does not seem edifying.

>   G.   1:21-28 And they go to
>   Capernaum; and forthwith on
>   the Sabbath, going into the
>   synagogue, he taught. And
>   they were amazed at his
>   teaching, for he was teach-
>   ing them as one having author-
>   ity and not as the scribes.
>   And forthwith there was in

> their synagogue a man in an
> unclean spirit, and he cried
> out, saying, "What have you
> to do with us, Jesus Nazarene?
> Do you come to destroy us? I
> know you, who you are, the
> holy one of God." And Jesus
> rebuked him, [saying,] "Be
> silent, and come out of him."
> And the unclean spirit, con-
> vulsing him and crying with
> a loud voice, came out of him.
> And they were all astonished,
> so as to discuss among them-
> selves, saying "What is this?
> new teaching with authority;
> and he commands the unclean
> spirits, and they obey him."
> And forthwith his fame went
> out into the whole region of
> Galilee.

The recurrence of *forthwith* at the beginning of
this passage seems nothing but a mindless stylistic reflex: its potential force is essentially cancelled by the steadying detail that it
was "on the Sabbath." The account of the exorcism is given immediately after the people's
positive response has been registered: surely
an appropriate sequence. Or so it seems, until
the exorcism is met with a questioning response
that begins by asking about a new teaching. We
had seemingly been assured earlier that they
were positively impressed with his teaching.
Why a question about it now?——especially at a

moment when the subject surely ought to be the
exorcism. It is possible, if one wants to give
Mark a generous benefit of doubt, to read the
passage as if the last question is roughly
equivalent to "What have we here?! What shall
we make of this new teaching when we see that
it is not only impressive of itself but even
supported by the power to command even unclean
spirits?" But that is a benefit which Mark has
not yet earned, nor will earn subsequently.
Mark has apparently telescoped two different
stories, one about the reaction to the teaching,
another about the reaction to the exorcism. He
has not done it gracefully. The reporting is
irretrievably awkward: one may divine what Mark
meant to say, but there is no defending his way
of saying it.

> H.   1:29-31 And forthwith, having
>   come out of the synagogue, he
>   [they?] went into the house of
>   Simon and Andrew, with James
>   and John. Now Simon's mother-
>   in-law lay with a fever, and
>   forthwith they spoke to him
>   about her. And approaching,
>   he raised her, taking her hand;
>   and the fever left her, and
>   she served them.

Mark took the newly enlisted disciples to Caper-
naum in verse 21, but abandoned them in the
same verse as he concentrated on the entrance

of Jesus into the Synagogue. Now, happily, he
remembers them again. Less felicitously, he
picks up James and John with his customary and
pointless "forthwith" and neglects to say
whether Simon and Andrew, to whose house they
proceed, are members of the party: presumably,
identifying the house by their names is supposed to be the equivalent of acknowledging
their presence, though it is probably more accurate to suggest that Mark, having mentioned
their names, simply failed to notice that he
did so in a way that did not necessarily mean
that they were there. After another needless
"forthwith" (and a carelessly unspecified antecedent for "*they* spoke"), the rest flows smoothly enough, even if it may seem fussily detailed
to say that "approaching, he raised her, taking
her hand."

> I.   1:32-34 Evening having come,
> when the sun set, they brought
> to him all those who were sick
> and those who were possessed
> with demons; and the whole
> city was gathered at the door.
> And he healed many who were
> sick with various maladies,
> and cast out many demons; and
> he did not allow the demons to
> speak, because they knew him.

The point of specifying that the sick were not
brought for healing until sundown was origin-

ally, one presumes, so that the Sabbath would
not be infringed; but Mark does not say so, and
has just reported two Sabbath cures which no
one seemed to consider irregular, even though
one took place in the Synagugue itself. The
force and meaning of this detail is accordingly
dulled, and the Gentile reader may be excused
if he innocently presumes that Mark has merely
allowed time for Jesus' healing reputation to
spread sufficiently. No one need object to the
hyperbole of the whole city gathered at the
door, but there is something unsatisfying in
the laconic report that Jesus did not permit
the demons to speak. Who expected them to
speak, in the first place? And why is it important for them not to speak? Luke handles the
parallel story with attention to narrative
needs: he first has the demons acknowledge that
Jesus is the Son of God, and then has Jesus rebuke them and forbid them to speak because they
know that he is the Messiah. Not ideally
crafted exposition, but satisfactory and effective: Luke has at least given an occasion for
Jesus' command of silence (the demons had said
something, and evidently something Jesus did
not want to have them say) and has represented
Jesus as specifying what they are not permitted
to say, clearly implying that the motive was to

keep the demons from revealing or publicizing
Jesus's Messianic identity. Mark simply has
Jesus not permit the demons to speak at all,
adding the lame explanation "because they knew
him." One can understand why some textual witnesses have tried to improve on the sense by
adding "to be the Christ," since that at least
partially clarifies what the point of keeping
them silent might be. Even that addition does
not quite rescue the text, however, since we
must make a considerable leap of inference to
conclude that if they had been allowed to speak,
they would have disclosed Jesus' Messiahship
and that he did not want this to happen: Luke
gets around that problem by having them speak
and be hushed about what they say, but the Marcan text, even with the improvement made by
later manuscripts, is weak and vague. Superficially, it may seem that Mark can use a sort
of shorthand here, counting on us to recall the
silencing of another demon a few verses earlier;
but in fact, a close look at verse 25 reveals
that there is no indication that it is being re-
buked or silenced for the offense of identifying Jesus as the Holy One of God. That demon
speaks, and is told to shut up and get out: it
does not obviously matter what he has said.
Thus the later instance of not allowing the

demons to speak "because they knew him" is extremely oblique if it is meant to convey "because they knew that he was the Messiah and
would say so if allowed to speak, which was
contrary to his wishes." As a sketchy reminder
of motives and situations which we know from
other sources (which is the way we usually read
it), this curtailed account will do; but as an
original, it is not good technique.

> J. 1:35-39 And early, while it
>   was still quite dark, rising,
>   he went out and departed into
>   an uninhabited place, and
>   prayed there. And Simon and
>   those with him searched him
>   out; and having found him, they
>   say to him that "Everyone is
>   seeking you." And he says to
>   them, "Let us go elsewhere,
>   into the neighboring towns, so
>   that I may proclaim there also;
>   for it is for this that I came
>   forth." And he went [was?]
>   proclaiming in their synagogues,
>   in the whole of Galilee, and
>   casting out the demons.

No important blunder mars this pericope, even
if "he went out, and departed" is original Mark:
the second verb can be stylistically justified
as the beginning of a new narrative phase, the
first verb being the conclusion of the previous
one. All the same, the pattern of events is
mildly unsatisfying. Jesus arises early, and

departs; Simon and the others search for him,
and announce that everyone is seeking him. The
flow of the text suggests that Simon's search
follows Jesus' departure at no great interval,
yet something unreported seems to have happened
in the meantime to occasion the search—everyone
is seeking Jesus. (This can hardly mean the
crowds of the previous evening, since that would
be no news at all; yet if it is a new crowd of
the morning, why aren't we told about it? Luke's
version of the story expressly narrates that
the crowds went looking for Jesus. That works
somewhat more smoothly.)

> K. 1:40-45 And a leper comes to
> him, beseeching him and kneel-
> ing, saying to him that "If
> you will, you can make me
> clean." And, being moved with
> pity [being angry?], stretching
> out his hand, he touched [him]
> and says to him, "I will: be
> made clean." And forthwith the
> leprosy left him, and he was
> made clean. And having rumbled
> at him, forthwith he drove him
> forth and says to him, "See
> that you do not say anything to
> anyone, but go show yourself to
> the priest, and offer for your
> cleansing the things Moses com-
> manded, for a witness to them."
> But he, going out, began to
> proclaim considerably, and to
> spread the word abroad, so that
> he was no longer able to enter

> openly into town, but was
> out in uninhabited places;
> and they came to him from
> all over.

The transition from 39 to 40 is awkward: Mark
follows a general summing-up couched in a past
tense with a specific instance set in the present. One could understand presenting things
the other way around, but this order reads oddly, as does the repeated shifting back and forth
from present to past to present to past within
the passage at hand. More awkwardly still,
Mark relates that Jesus cured **the** leper, rumbled
at him in some unclear way, and straightaway
sent him off—and then he pauses to report to us
(in the present tense) the content of Jesus'
orders, after mentioning that the man has been
sent away, making the transition with a mere
"and." Obviously, the graceful moment to specify the orders is before the definitive dismis-
sal; this is clumsy afterthought. The final
verse concludes the story by having the leper
unaccountably contravene the command given him,
with no attempt to explain why, and then an-
nounces that for this reason Jesus could no
longer enter a city openly. How does this conclusion follow? Obliquely, the final words,
testifying to Jesus' undiminished popularity,
may be taken to suggest that his reason for

keeping to deserted places was that he would be
mobbed by ebthusiasts should he enter cities.
But it might also be read as darkly alluding to
some point of disfavor that might make it dangerous for Jesus to appear in cities, as is eventually the case in Jerusalem. Mark does not give
us much guidance, and the meaning of the event
is left importantly ambiguous (is this a new
height for Jesus' career, or the beginning of a
serious decline?). It doesn't seem to matter
much to Mark: he is about to send Jesus back to
a major city anyway, in the very next verse,
after only "some days." How seriously can we
take the matter then? Or, perhaps more to the
point, how seriously can we take the narrator?

II. THE CHAPTER AS A WHOLE

The individual units of Mark's first
chapter are inescapably faulty. Is it possible
to claim distinction for his writing by arguing
that the overall sequence manifests a subtle
control and purposeful design that is wanting
in the particular parts? I do not think so.
To be sure, the first chapter makes a strong impression and serves effectively as a beginning
to the rest of the Gospel. But this has mainly
to do with the impressiveness of the events

recounted, not the way in which Mark's redaction orchestrates their possibilities. The beginning is abrupt and strong with appropriate solemnities, and moves compellingly into the high points of the ministry of John——only to lose impetus, energy, and continuity by pausing to detail John's clothing and diet. Appealing again to the previous momentum, Mark then returns to the more impressive aspects of John's work, falters briefly with the flat and matter-of fact introduction of Jesus into the scene, and again rises to the powerful events succeeding Jesus' baptism. The overall impression thus far is excellent, though the lapses in momentum are mildly disappointing and without apparent purpose. The temptation episode is something of a letdown, too plainly uttered and too cryptically compressed to be a satisfactory immediate sequel to the grand details of the post-baptismal events. The beginnings of Jesus' preaching are effectively presented, but the transition to the call of the first disciples suddenly and pointlessly changes pace, telling the episode with fussy detail that would have been welcome in the temptation story or in the account of Jesus' first preachings but seems oddly lavished on these relatively insignificant aspects of a less momentous event. Why place

the call of the disciples here, if they are not
to be involved in the next episode? How do
they relate to it? Mark neglects these obvious
points of continuity to plunge into the arresting account of the teaching and the exorcism,
concluding with a curiously incoherent conflation of the people's reaction to his teaching
(previously unqualifiedly positive, now unaccountably questioning) and their reaction to
the exorcism—a less effective order of presentation than the reverse would have been. So
far, the thrust has been strong, with minor
lapses. In some respects, there has been a
crescendo. Now suddenly Mark turns to the homely and domestic cure of Simon's mother-in-law,
an anticlimactic episode that again oddly spends
minor details that might have been effective in
the previous tale but tends to slow and dilute
the strength of this one. Isolated, the treatment of this cure is apt enough; but in context,
it is an inexplicable change of pace. The
coming of the crowd restores the earlier scale
and verve, somewhat slowed by the aftermath of
the cures, but brought to a ringing general conclusion—which is immediately diminished by a
particular story of a leper's cure that ends in
a confusing consequence that is dramatically
presented but casually abandoned in the subse-

quent verse.

The flow of the story is not silllfully
organized. The overall sequence is not likely
to be Mark's invention: its high points (the
account of John, the baptism of Jesus, the beginning of Jesus' ministry, the encounter with
the Synagogue at Caparnaum) must inevitably be
given in a Gospel drawn from this tradition,
and in that order. If Mark is responsible for
inserting the other materials in their Marcan
places, he has not much advantaged his narrative by doing so; if he is responsible for
their specific narrative character, he has not
taken much care to blend them effectively with
their surroundings. If he has merely passed on
more or less accurately a total pattern inherited from traditional telling, and the styles
that came with the various parts, then the deficiencies in sequential effect must be attributed to other and anonymous agents: but there
can be no doubt that there are deficiencies.
The obvious successes are essentially the successes of the major events themselves. The ma-
trix into which they have been case is clumsy,
redeemed by no apparent thematic, cumulative,
rhythmic, or other hidden principle of coher-
ence. It is the stuff of very ordinary story-
telling—not egregiously incompetent, but normally clumsy, with a few moments of creative

gracefulness displayed along its generally routine and plodding way.

III.   CONCLUSIONS

Some of the foregoing criticisms have admittedly been petty, a few perhaps cavilling.
I do not mean to complain, and I agree that it
is somewhat unfair to blame Mark for blunders,
or to read his work as if he is to be held
scrupulously responsible for every turn of
phrase.   In fact, that is precisely my point.
The cumulative effect of this kind of close
reading seems to me to be a clear demonstration
that this is very ordinary, homely, untrained
prose, full of the same stylistic sloppinesses
and clumsy mismanagement of basic storytelling
techniques that one expects to find in unsophis-
ticated writing in all times and places.   It
should not be read as if it is the product of
masterful perceptiveness displaying itself in
deft finesse and subtle suggestion: it is indeed possible to read it that way, just as it
is possible to read ominously between the lines
of an innocent letter, or to see implicit complaint or compliment where there is no such matter, or to give great deliberate weight to an
ignorantly misused word.   But it is not appropriate to do so.   That is to impose a false

frame of expectations. Proper close reading
should adapt itself accommodatingly to the real
character of the text in question. What I have
attempted to establish is that the character of
this text, as evidenced by both the individual
parts and the overall sequential flow of its
opening section, suggests that it is the product of a rather ordinarily clumsy writer, probably working on materials that had come to him
in ordinarily clumsy form. There is little basis for inferring either inexorable laws of formal development or a high level of purposeful
redactional control: the intrusion of clumsiness is too pervasive to permit a reading to
presume such rigorous rationalities as these.

        The first chapter of Mark's Gospel is
not exceptional in this regard. Similar evidences lie ready to hand in all the other chap-
ters. But rather than try your patience with a
similar *seriatim* commentary on the remainder, I
would like to give a slightly more detailed
illustration of the Marcan capacities in story-
telling by taking three representative examples
from elsewhere in the Gospel: a brief pericope,
in which Mark undermines his main intent by attempting a clarifying explanation that back-
fires; a longer pericope that shows some glim-
merings of his positive creativity among his
somewhat incoherent shufflings of routine story-

telling motifs; and another brief passage in
which he employs standard devices of elaboration in a manner that leads to nearly total
mystification and the complete obfuscation of
what was probably the main point of his source.
I shall then turn to one of the larger and theologically more significant redactional themes
of Mark's Gospel, in an attempt to account for
it more satisfactorily than hitherto, through
the interpretive application of the principle
of clumsiness.

CHAPTER THREE

THREE PERICOPES

A survey of Mark's first chapter suggests that he inherits, and continues, a tradition of ordinarily clumsy transmission of stories. Once one has achieved accurate bearings on the standards of control that obtain in this tradition, it becomes possible to apply this adjusted frame of expectations to read still more closely. When sufficient allowance is made for the operation of clumsiness both in Mark's antecedents and in his own handling of his received material, it may be possible to assess more accurately just how the most recent layers of tradition are being reworked in the Marcan text—just what it is that Mark, or some immediate predecessor, was attempting to do in forming the Marcan version of the story, and just where and how we may account for that version's peculiarities by acknowledging that things went describably wrong.

The most convenient place to experiment
is, of course, in instances where we have access
to alternative versions of the same basic story.
I shall therefore deal with three examples of
Marcan stories that also appear elsewhere, all
three in Matthew and one in Luke as well. But
before doing so, I would like to comment briefly
on some of the presuppositions I do not make,
and some that I do.

Not long ago, it was commonly presumed
that one of the permanently assured results of
New Testament criticism was the Two-Source or
Two-Document Hypothesis—i.e., that the Gospels
of Matthew and Luke were composed with reference
to two shared sources, the hypothetical Q and
the tangible Gospel of Mark. Synoptic criticism
normally took axiomatically for granted that
differences between most stories shared by Mark
on the one hand and Matthew or Luke on the other
were best understood by supposing that the latter (and, *ex hypothesei*, later) Gospels were
using Mark and departing from his version of
the story for special and potentially discernible purposes of their own or of their communi-
ties. Occasionally, a voice (most notably that
of William Farmer) would cry out in otherwise
deserted critical territory that Mark is not
necessarily the earliest Gospel and the major
source of the other two Synoptics, but such

voices normally went largely unheeded.   To
study Matthew or Luke, one presupposed Mark as
source.

        This question has been firmly reopened.
One can hardly say that the earlier axiom has
been withdrawn, for contemporary New Testament
criticism still generally uses it, and some
prominent scholars of the Synoptic Gospels consider the matter still essentially closed, and
not worth reconsidering. But the question has
decidedly been reopened: the founding arguments
of the Two-Source Hypothesis are being subject-
ed to new critical scrutiny, which finds them
flawed; the assumptions are being weighed and
found somewhat wanting; the awkward evidences
that were once considered maverick and puzzling
exceptions are being tested as possible keys to
a revised theory of Gospel origins; the objec-
tions to alternative theories are being carefully explored and tested, and tend not to be
sustained.

        I am not *parti pris* on this issue. I am
neither prepared nor inclined to defend the assumption of Marcan priority; neither am I dis-
posed to consider that assumption definitively
disqualified. I settle for recognizing that
the question has in fact been effectively reopened, and take comfort in knowing that it is
in the hands of scholars much better qualified

to deal with it—and much more interested in
its outcome—than I. The attentive reader will
have noticed that I have already compared Mark's
stories with those of Matthew and Luke, and
that I have found this comparison to be to
Mark's disadvantage. The *very* attentive reader
will have noticed that I have remained proced-
urally agnostic about the implications. Mark's
version is often inferior to that of one or
both of his colleagues. That does not mean,
however, that they are improving directly on
what he wrote: a better version does not mean
a later one, nor does a longer version, nor a
more sophisticated version, nor a more solemn
version. I have tried to say why I think it
reasonable to distrust hypothesized rigorous
laws of development, and why I am disinclined
to suppose that the texts in question have been
formed under consistent and purposeful control.
As a result of this distrust and disinclination,
I am left uncertain about how Mark relates to
Matthew and Luke. I suspect that the origins
of the Synoptic Gospels are much more complex
and intricate than criticism is accustomed to
imagine, or would credit if proposed. When I
compare Mark with his fellows in the course of
this chapter, therefore, it is only to high-
light achieved alternative ways of doing what
in general Mark was setting out to do, so that

he might be set in perspective. But the perspective in question is not one of direct deri-
vation, in either direction: it is the perspective of perennial clumsiness.

I.   THE CURSING OF THE FIG TREE (11:12-14,20)

> And the next day, as they were
> coming out of Bethany, he was
> hungry: and seeing a fig-tree
> from afar, having leaves, he
> went,—perhaps he will find
> something on it. And coming
> up to it, he found nothing but
> leaves, for it was not the
> season for figs. And respond-
> ing, he said to it: "May no one
> eat fruit from you from now
> unto the age." And his dis-
> ciples were hearing.... And
> in the morning, passing along,
> they saw the fig tree, withered
> up from the roots.

It is instructive to compare this with Matthew's
version of the same story (21:18-20: "But in
the morning, returning to the city, he was hungry and seeing a single fig tree by the way, he
came to it, and found nothing on it but leaves
alone, and he said to it, 'Nevermore any fruit
be produced by you unto the age.' And the fig
tree withered instantly.") Matthew's sequence
is economically right, pared down to the necessary details with little left over. He gives
the time and the setting, both of which are

supportive of the next and motivating detail of
Jesus' hunger. At that point, having set the
problem, he introduces the potential solution,
identifying the tree in a way that suggests
that it is the only potential source of food in
sight, and briefly reminding us that we are
still en route. He then moves Jesus to it, and
registers the disappointing discovery with an
appropriate flourish. Jesus reacts vindictive-
ly, with instant results. One may raise questions about what Matthew then does with this
episode, but the story itself is excellently
set forth.

Mark's version is considerably less
skillful. As a scene-setting, the specification of a point of departure is less relevant
to the character of the story than Matthew's
specification of a destination. The detail
"from afar" is not altogether necessary, but
helps both prepare the expectation (even from a
distance, one could see that it was in leaf,
ergo is eligible for fruit as well) and explain
Jesus' failure to discern the absence of fruit
at the time of sighting. Still, this is less
efficient than Matthew's version: fussy provi-
sion for these considerations is unnecessary,
since the mentioning of the fig tree after the
hunger will establish the possibility of figs,
and Jesus' approach to it will confirm our sup-

position that he had reason to think there
might be figs; the detail of the leaves is oddly overspecific, and robs the eventual rhetorical flourish "nothing but leaves" of some of
its dash. (It is not improbable that this detail is in fact nothing more than a displaced
remembrance of that eventual touch, an anticipatory false start that sets up antecedent conditions that do not need mentioning.) The account of Jesus' approach tells us nothing we do
not otherwise know, but is a winsome emphasis
that helps build anticipation effectively. The
next bit follows smoothly and logically, as in
Matthew, and Mark successfully plays his trump
phrase, "he found nothing but leaves." But
here Mark pauses, fatally, to attend to an apparent incongruity. Jesus went to look for
figs, but his quest is frustrated. How do we
account for this unsuccess? Mark (or, as always, his source) may have been thinking of
some indecorum in attributing a failed project
to Jesus, or he may merely have been thinking
of the homely and superficial cognitive disso-
nance that arises from expecting something and
not getting it. At any rate, he feels obliged
to account for this surprise by adding an explanation: it was not the season for figs. He
then plunges on, but from this point there is

no recovering his tale, not even when he thoughtfully provides the disciples with ear-witness status so that we may be sure that they are in a position to grasp the significance of the withered tree the next day (for we are prepared to take that for granted). It was not the season for figs! True to the perennial habits of the partially creative but clumsy storyteller, he has perceived and resolved a trivial and superficial localized difficulty without noticing that his solution to the problem has made hash of the overall tale—for now Jesus must seem inexplicably silly to look for figs out of season, and outrageously unjust to punish the tree for its obedience to the ordained times and seasons. However circumspect Mark has been about certain random minor effects, the disciplining consideration of the overall story and its needs has eluded him, and that careless obliviousness has, whether or not he has any inkling of it, been ruinous.

II. THE GERASENE DEMONIAC (5:1-17)

The longer example I wish to consider is Mark's handling of the tale of the Gerasene demoniac (or is it Gadarene? Mark is unlikely to be in a position to know or care which of the settings is more compatible with the geo-

graphical details of his story, and it is at
least possible that the minor reading "Gergesene"
is his own concoction out of fuzzy recollection,
subsequently corrected by those who knew better).[21] This is a story that is somewhat incoherent in all three Synoptic versions, and my
side-references to Matthew and Luke are again
not meant to suggest that either of them has
preserved an "uncorrupted" or "authentic" version, but merely to illustrate from concrete and
non-hypothetical examples some of the ways in
which Mark might better have commanded the telling of his tale.

       After an orderly introduction, Mark sup-
plies (with his customary "forthwith" [euthus],
in at least some witnesses) the encounter of
Jesus with the demoniac. Having introduced the
key figure, he goes on (quite properly, if un-
necessarily) to add the exciting and grotesque
information that the man dwelt habitually among
the tombs, and could not be restrained even
with chains. Matthew (who provides two demon-
iacs, for no apparent reason other than to just-
ify the plural verbs which in Mark and Luke
arise from the Legion of demons inhabiting the
single demoniac) is content to register merely
that the possessed came forth from the tombs,
and then continues the story (8:28); Luke adds,
though as a later afterthought detail (8:29),

that the demoniac had been guarded, bound with
chains and fetters which he broke. But Mark's
story-telling imagination is fired with rare
enthusiasm, and he pauses to expatiate on the
Gothic motifs: not content with the adequately
suggestive remark that the man could no longer
be restrained by anyone, even with chains, he
elaborates a brief flashback history: "for he
had been many times bound with fetters and
chains, and the chains had been burst by him
and the fetters broken, and no one had power to
subdue him" (5:4). He then further embroiders
the potentially eerie setting of the tombs,
with forceful emphasis ("and always, night and
day, he was in the tombs") and caps off the
biographical information with striking additional detail: "...he was in the tombs and in
the mountains, crying out and cutting himself
with stones" (5:5). This is not very directly
to the point of the story, but at least raises
the dramatic stakes somewhat, and what it loses
in economy it gains in vitality and thrill.
Evidently, either Mark has finally found his
own element, or he has been listening to someone who had.

But eventually, he must get on with the
central business of the story. Forgetting that
he has already said that Jesus and the demoniac
had met (*hupēntēsen*, 5:2), Mark now has the

demoniac see Jesus at a distance. This is in
itself, aside from that inconsistency, an effective narrative detail, much imitated by dramatic cinematography; but it is purchased at
the price of certain problems. Mark must now
move the man to Jesus' vicinity; and so, although the logic of the situation would presumably motivate his demonic possessors to flee,
he has the man run to meet Jesus. Luke, who
has not had to deal with the problem of distance, now has the man fall down, as in submis-
sion (*prosepesen*, 8:28). Mark has evidently
received some such detail, but has misconstrued
the basis of its narrative appropriateness: accordingly, he has the demoniac rather less
plausibly fall down in reverence (*proskunēsen*,
5:6). After reporting the man's (or the demon's?) plea to be left alone, Mark then gives
in a lame parenthesis the command to which this
had been a response: "(For he had said to him,
'Come out, unclean spirit, from the man.')" (5:
8). Then come the question and answer about
the spirit's name—a memorably haunting detail
much in keeping with Mark's verve about the
other eerie elements of the story, even if also
a sidetrack from the main emphasis. Mark now
shows an understandable (though theoretically
resolvable) confusion about whether the man's
verbs should be singular or plural. Before he

finds a stabilizing formula for this in verse
12, he treats us to the charmingly homely request that the demons not be driven "out of the
district"—and a comparison of Mark's *exō tēs
chōras* with Luke's "into the abyss" (*eis tēn
abusson*, 8:31) is an edifying reminder that a
measure of rude simplemindedness in story-telling can sometimes at least secure pleasing effects that are lost to sober correctness.

Suddenly the swine are introduced into
the scene, and the demons come up with a count-
er-proposal. It is granted promptly and flatly,
in three words, as if Jesus takes pity on them
and declines to press his advantage; but if
initially unaccountable, this is not allowed
to be bothersome for long: Mark forthwith resolves the difficulty by destroying the swine.
With them, presumably, we are to suppose the
demons also perished; at any rate, their part
of the story is abandoned as if it were finished.
The happy irony of their having requested the
arrangements for their own demise is satisfying
enough to obscure the possible questions about
what made the swine so suicidal (presumably demonic madness; and to an audience of Jews and
fellow-travellers, the satisfying appropriateness of self-liquidating pigs would further
distance the theoretical problem), and whether
demons can really drown with their hosts. There

has been a little narrative juggling, but it
appears that at least in this mode, Mark knows
what a story-teller can do. One can readily
forgive him the belatedly sensational detail
that the now deceased swine numbered two thousand.

     The swineherds, previously unacknowl-
edged, spread the news and the crowd gathers.
With an arbitrary but not inappropriate shift
of tense from past to present, the residents of
the city and the villages "came out to see what
it is that has happened; and they come to Jesus
and see the demoniac sitting down, clothed, and
in his senses" (5:14-15). Mark does not worry
about where the clothes came from, any more
than he worries about lapse of time while the
swineherds alert the nearby towns and the towns-
men collect at the site. But then, Mark (unlike Luke) had not bothered to tell us previously that the man was naked, although he had obviously remembered that the eventual clothing
was a significant suggestive detail in the version he had heard. Those who have seen now
tell "how it happened to the demoniac, and
about the swine" (5:16). The specification of
themes is of course unnecessary for us, but an
effectively economical encapsulation of the act
of telling, and a welcome final reminder of the

highlights of this lively story. The inhabi-
tants show disappointingly little interest in
the one who has worked these wonders. They do
not ask who he is, or how he comes to have such
powers, or what brings him to this place. They
merely "entreat him to depart from their re-
gions" (5:17), which is a commendably restrained
response to two thousand drowned pigs, but shows
a distressing lack of evangelical curiosity.
Not that Mark shows any distress; he delivers
the report in a matter-of-fact way, has Jesus
decline the ex-demoniac's request to be allowed
to accompany him, and ends the tale with a
graceful and fitting coda on the witness effectively spread by the grateful man. Admittedly,
this is totally out of keeping with the policy
Jesus has followed on the other side of the Sea
of Galilee concerning publicity arising from
cures, and rather inconsistent with injunctions
to follow him, but brings the story to an appropriate conclusion nevertheless.

Mark has here surrendered his characteristic brevity, and entered into the tale with
considerable vivacity. The story contains various of the usual bumblings of story-telling,
but they are overwhelmed by the lively and creative touches that leave Matthew's version
looking drab by comparison. Is this Mark's own
accomplishment, or is it essentially his appre-

ciative appropriation of the achievements of
one of his predecessors? I myself have no idea;
but in either event, two things are worth noting.
On the one hand, Mark here enshrines among his
other stories a bright example of the teller's
art: he cannot be accused of having been unex-
posed to the dramatic techniques of narration,
and may here have shown that he can employ them
creditably himself. And on the other hand, he
has given us a story, within the bosom of his
Gospel, in which the memorable elaborative attention is lavished not on Jesus, or Jesus'
message, or even on the miraculous cure itself,
but rather on a Gothic madman and a herd of
stampeding swine. The supposition that Mark,
and the Synoptic tradition in which he stands,
always kept a steady focus on proclaiming the
Gospel of Jesus Christ, and subordinated all
other values and interests to this end, must
meet with sobering second thoughts when one
reads the tale of the demonic Legion and sees
who steals the show.

III.   THE LEAVEN OF THE PHARISEES (8:14-21)

> And they neglected to take
> loaves, and except for one
> loaf they did not have any
> with them in the ship. And
> he charged them, saying,
> "Look out: beware of the

leaven of the Pharisees,
and the leaven of Herod."
And they discussed with
one another that they do
not have loaves. And,
knowing, he says to them,
"Why are you discussing
that you do not have loaves?
Do you not yet understand
nor comprehend? Do you
have a dulled heart? Having
eyes, do you not see? And
do you not remember when
I broke the five loaves
for the five thousand, how
many baskets full of fragments you took up?" They
say to him: "Twelve."
"When the seven for the
four thousand, how many
hampers full of fragments
did you take up?" And they
say: "Seven." And he said
to them, "Do you not understand yet?"

The third example, involving more specifically redactional phenomena, is this brief
appendix to the pericope concerning the leaven
of the Pharisees, for which Matthew also records a version. (Luke gives us the utterance
about the leaven, with an explanation, but does
not record the further adventure which it occasions in Matthew and Mark.) Mark's tale begins
with the disciples reasoning among themselves
that Jesus' words were spoken because they had
no bread—not altogether accurate, since al-

though Mark (like Matthew) has anticipated this
conversation by establishing that they had neglected to bring bread, he (unlike Matthew) curiously adds that they had a single loaf with
them (8:14—plausibly, a mishandling of a detail
that originally ran "had *not* a single loaf").
Jesus knows what they are saying (a slightly
awkward detail, since Mark does not quite either confirm or deny that there is anything significant in his knowing this) and reproves them.
Here Mark suddenly bursts into verve. The accusations tumble out in a sweeping tirade: do
you not perceive, do you not understand, is
your heart stupified, do you not see with your
eyes, do you not hear with your ears, do you
not remember? Matthew takes us more directly
toward the point: do you not grasp or remember
the miracle of the loaves? (16:9-10). But in
the effulgence of Mark's general indictment of
their insensitivity, there is no specific direction. Indeed, there is the virtual implication that an appeal to a particular instance
might obscure the exasperatingly general nature
of their opacity. The appeal to the loaves
thus seems to come into the picture as an illustration or as an attempt at rescuing them from
their dullness, but it does not seem to be (as
Matthew makes it) the specific reason for the
charges just made.

The little catechism which Jesus puts
them through at this point is evidently intended to throw some light on things for them. The
questions are clear, and the disciples clearly
produce the right answers. The reader may well
empathize with the hopelessly obtuse pupils
when Jesus then closes off the matter with "Do
you not yet understand?" Evidently, somewhere
in those simple questions and correct answers
is hidden the key. But what is it? What is
the significance of *twelve* baskets and *seven*
baskets that they should bring great insight?
Poor blockheads, they don't get it. Uneasily,
the reader may also note that he himself is
just as much in the dark, despite his post-resurrection advantage over the puzzled disciples.

As it stands, the story seems self-defeating, unless its point were that proper insight is quite beyond all of us and yet required all the same. What has gone wrong?
Matthew's version, I believe, suggests the solution. For although Matthew seems to have had
some trouble with the story himself—and admittedly might himself have given intelligibility to a tale that came to him as unfathomable
as Mark's—his treatment makes sense of the
whole episode. The disciples think that Jesus
is obliquely criticizing them for not bringing
bread. Jesus takes this to be evidence of a

lack of faith, and presses on them the implications of having distributed five loaves to five
thousand people and having large quantities left
over. The lesson is clear enough. Of course he
could not have been worrying about bread! He
has just given the most obvious public demonstration that he can produce bread in vast abundance
when it is needed. Jesus then reinforces the
point by saying explicitly that they ought to
have realized that he was not speaking about
bread when he spoke of leaven, and the disciples
finally grasp his metaphor.

     Mark's version gets somewhat sidetracked
from what must have been its main line of development when he becomes carried away with Jesus'
elaborate rebuke, but its real breakdown comes
with the questions and answers. Mark has presumably known a version rather like Matthew's,
in which Jesus refers to the baskets of fragments as evidence that he can not only supply
bread, but even in great superfluity: Don't you
remember the five loaves for the five thousand,
and how many basketfuls you gathered? Mark
heard the question, but missed its function.
Remembering that Jesus had asked a question involving how many baskets there were in the two
incidents, he then reconstructs the question
for his own retelling—but not having quite
comprehended the story in the first place,

he understands the question to be one *about* how
many baskets there were, rather than merely *involving* how many baskets there were. Having
thus interpreted the question, he can see no
reason why the disciples should not answer it.
They know the answers, after all; and the small
bit of dialogue enlivens the story. Hence we
have two separate questions, each one responded
to in accordance with the facts he has already
given earlier. Mark has now arrived at the end
of his story, and remembers that Jesus, after
posing his apparently telling question, had
then insisted that they ought to get the point.
He therefore has Jesus say so. But since Mark
himself does not understand what the point is,
he cannot have Jesus specify (as he does in
Matthew's version, 16:11) "How is it that you
do not understand *that I was not talking about
bread?*" He must content himself with the general question, "Do you not yet understand?,"
and move on to his next story.

Unlike most of the weaknesses in Mark's
story-telling, the difficulties in this pericope arise not from clumsiness in his technique
but from a sheet opacity of his own. Mark has
passed the story on without having understood
it. His reconstruction suggests what he had
carried away from his hearing of it: Jesus was
threateningly vexed at his followers' inability

to understand, mysteriously asked some seemingly superficial but evidently profound questions
about the loaves and baskets, and appeared sur-
prised that after that they still did not understand. Misconstrued in this way, the incident
has a hauntingly mysterious and unsettling character. That aura further reinforces its internal suggestion that this incident was considered
by Jesus a particularly significant case of un-
comprehension on the disciples' part. The story
thus seems clearly important, and ought therefore to be included in one's collection. And
so, reconstructing it more or less in the image
and likeness of his recollected impression,
Mark supposes that he has passed it on.

He has not taken it lightly. On the
contrary, its elusiveness commands his respect-
ful attention. He has gathered from it that
somewhere in the incident of the loaves and baskets is a revelation of some deep truth about
Jesus which his disciples had not readily
grasped because of dullwittedness. And therefore, when he reports their amazement on the occasion of Jesus' walking on water and stilling
the wind, he solemnly adds a reference to this
mysterious touchstone: "They did not yet understand about the loaves, for their heart was
stupified" (6:52). Mark probably supposes that
he himself, as a Christian, somehow understands

the important truth about the loaves, although
he cannot put into words just how. From a
mystification, a mystery is born.[22]

IV. CONCLUSIONS

These three pericopes do more than confirm the impressions left by Mark's first chapter. They do indeed provide such confirmation
—further evidence of a style of mind and of
composition that are, as the saying goes, no
better than they ought to be. But more than
this, they show the realization of what the
first chapter gives only as shadowy possibility.
There we see that the redactional control, or
want of it, is such as to raise the possibility
of disaster. Here we see actual disasters.
There we see a certain Marcan capacity to be
distracted momentarily from the central considerations; here we see more sustained digression
and compromise of values. If these three pericopes do not show us much about Mark that had
not already been hinted through his opening
pages, they show what it can cost.

They also, I believe, allow us a clearer
glimpse into the purposes and strategies which,
clumsily handled, give rise to strange and be-
musing results. The next chapter will attempt
one more such investigation, on a still larger

scale, in which I shall try to disentangle intelligibly the effects of pre-Marcan and Marcan
clumsiness in the management of a larger theological and historical motif.

CHAPTER FOUR

THE ESOTERIC TEACHING

Mark's treatment of the leaven of the
Pharisees is particularly worth keeping in mind
in pursuing other investigations in the Gospel
of Mark. It reminds us that the effect of
clumsiness lies not merely in the deformations
that come from carelessness and inadvertence;
sometimes the redactor's changes are deliberate,
his attention earnest, and yet similar misleading or confusing mischances occur, inflicted by
a zeal that outstrips editorial command. Even
when Marcan redactional touches are guided by
an intent, it does not follow that the policy
they pursue is fully intelligible or effective;
indeed, it does not follow that even Mark himself quite has a controlled understanding of
what he is after. Even in some of his most creative contributions, he is capable of sending
himself, with great earnestness, on a wild
goose chase. That, I believe, is essentially

what has happened in the case of the pericope
arising from the saying about the leaven of the
Pharisees. And that, I believe, is also a major consideration in some of the larger puzzling
hemes and motifs in Mark's Gospel.

       Tradition dealt with many pericopes,
many of them thematically or situationally related to one another. Customs of ordering entered the process of transmission, along with
other connective strategies. Mark created, or
inherited, a way of dividing the curse from the
next day's withered tree; and a way of linking
the disciples' reaction to Jesus' walking on
water with the miracles of the loaves (and both
with the leaven of the Pharisees). Still more
complex, and undoubtedly pioneered by others
before Mark, is the set of thematic and narrative connections established between the explained parable of the Sower, the characteristic
teaching in parables, the private instructions
to the disciples, and the mysterious idea of
hidden revelation. In this chapter, I deal
with one of the strangest of the compositional,
thematic, and theological problems of Mark's
Gospel, the problem of Jesus' Esoteric Teaching.
By a slow and careful unravelling of a large
and tangled problem, I hope to disclose how
clumsiness, in pre-Marcan tradition and in the
final redaction, made its influence felt in the

formation of a dreadful major misunderstanding.

I. THE PROBLEM OF ESOTERIC TEACHING

The problem of the Esoteric Teaching
thrusts itself upon us abruptly in Mark's
fourth chapter, by a sudden and peculiar set of
developments. Jesus has told the parable of
the Sower to the assembled crowd. He is subsequently alone, and the disciples inquire about
the parable. His reply is startling, claiming
that his teaching in parables is a way of blind-
ing outsiders and insuring their destruction—a
way of concealing the truth from the crowds,
while the inner circle of disciples will be
privileged to escape the general darkness, together with its dire consequences, and to know
the mystery deliberately withheld from others
(presumably through the explanations which Jesus
will give them, beginning now with an explanation of the parable of the Sower):

> And he said to them, "To you
> has been given the secret of
> the kingdom of God, but for
> those outside everything is
> in parables; so that they may
> indeed see but not perceive,
> and may indeed hear but not
> understand; lest they should
> turn again, and be forgiven"
> (4:11-12).

It is a curious policy: a public instruction

that does not instruct because of deliberate
concealment, supplemented by private disclosures
available only to the chosen few. The point of
teaching in public at all is hard to grasp, if
it is calculatedly unsuccessful; and the reason
for the concealment seems clearly unjust and
cruel. Those to whom it is given to know the
mystery of the Kingdom do so not by virtue of
clearheaded insight and faithful acceptance,
like the seed on good ground in the explicated
parable itself, but by special tutoring that is
denied to the others. And yet the special tutoring, once we get the parable explained, is
rather disappointingly bland and obvious, hardly seeming to be a dramatic exposition of the
mystery otherwise hidden.

        These are only a few of the immediately
puzzling features of this odd notion of special
esoteric teaching to the inner circle. There
are other oddities about it as well, of which I
will note here only two: (a) Parables are normally instruments of clarification, illustration,
illumination, not obfuscation. This is true
even for Mark. The parable of the sower is not
the first of the parables in Mark, for he has
introduced the term in the previous chapter, 3:
23: "And having called them, he said to them in
parables," and thereupon follow comparisons
with kingdoms and houses divided against them-

selves, and other parabolic sayings. It is obvious that these parables are meant to illuminate and establish a certain point, and that
their meaning is essentially clear. (b) Precisely in accordance with the lucid and effective
parables of chapter three, there is no sign
elsewhere in Mark's Gospel that the crowds were
ever mystified or left confused by the teaching
of Jesus. On the contrary, his teaching is
scandalously clear, even to his opponents; even
when he is speaking in parables, the consistent
impression is that he intends to be understood
and is understood. The only exceptions are,
ironically, the occasional instances in which
the closest disciples (or specifically the
Twelve) show a strange incapacity to comprehend
what appear to be fairly transparent metaphors
and even straightforward statements. The rest
of the Gospel, in short, tends to have the
crowds see and hear quite well, while the inner
circle has difficulties—nearly the opposite of
the policy strangely advanced in chapter four.
The motif of Esoteric Teaching is not only odd
in itself, but curiously inconsistent with the
Gospel at large.

Close scrutiny reveals that even chapter
four is not all of a piece, and is not consistently faithful to the esoteric teaching policy.
After the private explanation of the parable of

the Sower, Jesus continues with other parables
(not accompanied by explanations). Presumably,
the audience is still the closer disciples who
had heard the special explanation. Presumably,
it they to whom Mark refers in saying that "with
many such parables he spoke the word to them,
just as they were able to hear, and without a
parable he did not speak to them" (4:33-4)—except that he then adds "but privately, he explained all things to his disciples," and then
describes Jesus leaving the crowd and going
across the lake. Obviously, something is out of
place. It is not difficult to discover what it
is. At the beginning of the chapter, we are in
a public setting, with Jesus teaching the crowds
from a boat; toward the end of the chapter
(verse 33), we come to a summary conclusion that
unquestionably applies to the general teaching
to the crowds in parables, whereupon (35-6)
Jesus expresses the wish to cross the lake, and
his disciples row him away, leaving the crowd.
Verse 10, speaking of his being alone where the
disciples could consult him about the parable
of the Sower, seems to change the setting—but
somewhere between 10 and 33 the scene has shifted imperceptibly back to the public teaching of
the crowd by the lake and in parables. The private bypath with the closer disciples seems
clearly to have been an afterthought, imperfectly

carved out of public territory by a somewhat
clumsy redactor. Furthermore, the last portion
of verse 34, which returns to the subject of
private explanations to the disciples, is likewise out of keeping with its immediate surroundings. The preceding verse and a half say merely what the rest of Mark's Gospel would lead us
to believe: that Jesus spoke parables such that
the crowd could understand, *kathōs ēdunanto
akouein*. Further explanation is evidently unnecessary and a reference to it is against the
grain of this general discourse.

The difficulties of the esoteric teaching
are accordingly secondary, something added to
what had previously been the account of a public
parabolic teaching, and these difficulties are
localized in a very small portion of the chapter—for if one sets aside 10-13, dealing with
the setting and the introduction to the esoteric
disclosure, and 34b, which asserts that all
things were explained privately to the disciples,
all the rest flows coherently as the original
public teaching. These four and one-half verses,
mysteriously and clumsily grafted into a text to
which they are quite uncongenial, create the
problem of the esoteric teaching.

If the problem is created by these maverick verses of chapter four, it is nevertheless
partially sustained by later passages. The

motif of supplementary private explanation is
not confined to the fourth chapter. In chapter
seven, Jesus affirms that a man is not defiled
by what goes into him but rather by what comes
out of him; he then retires into a house, where
the disciples request and receive an explanation (7:14-23). In chapter nine, Jesus expels
the demon which his disciples could not master,
after which they retire to a house, where the
disciples ask him why they had been unsuccessful and are given a brief explanation (9:14-29).
After the following chapter's pronouncements on
marriage, the disciples are once more instructed
further on request, after they have withdrawn
to a house (10:1-12).[23]

　　　These passages only partially reaffirm
the esoteric policy, however. These latter two
instances involve special instruction that does
not involve the explanation of parables, the
one being an explanation of the disciples' exor-
cistic failure and the other a further elaboration on the implications of the teachings on
marriage. Only the first of the three examples
is in fact indisputably an instance of special
explanation of parables; it is therefore the
only visible followup in the Gospel to the
promises and generalizations about esoteric
teaching made in chapter four. Moreover, like
the explanation of the parable of the Sower, it

does not seem to offer any striking advantage
to the disciples; the original parable seems to
have been, and to have been received by the
crowds as, sufficiently intelligible all by itself.

There seems to be little reason for any
of these teachings to be given in private
asides, especially with the somewhat awkward
device of moving each time from the public setting into a house (a device which the other
Gospels do not employ for these particular
stories). It is doubtful that Mark could have
supposed that the reported private instructions
were indispensable to the understanding of Jesus' teaching, unless he engaged in another sort
of self-mystification and accepted on faith that
what seemed quite clear really wasn't. The examples he provides are too few and too routine
to give the impression of being the only adequate way to understand what Jesus taught. It
is similarly hard to suppose that Mark invented
them himself to provide illustrations of or
supporting evidence for the esoteric teaching
policy announced in chapter four, because they
are too blatantly inadequate for the task and
too marginal to the policy's main statement—
for in what sense are these supposed to be considered disclosures about the Kingdom? Surely
explanations invented as examples of such

crucial revelations would have been less banal,
and would have seemed more significantly revealing. On the other hand, Mark is not likely,
for similar reasons, to have invented the justi-
fying general policy of 4:10-13 as a way of
giving context and meaning to the specific instances of explanation which he intends to report. The explanations are not sufficiently impressive improvements to warrant such bold
claims as we find in 4:11 or such drastic consequences as are suggested in 4:12, especially
when the materials which Mark was handling contain such clear counter-evidence to not only the
historical probability but even the fundamental
plausibility of Jesus' ever having adopted such
a strategy. What then can we say about the
place and purpose of the Esoteric Teaching?
Where did it come from, and why did Mark make
use of it?

II.   THE BACKGROUND OF THE
ESOTERIC TEACHING MOTIF

The general tradition undoubtedly made it
clear to Mark that Jesus' teaching was characteristically in parables—for thus is he represented almost universally in surviving evidences.
I think it likely that Mark also received from
tradition a pre-Marcan version of the esoteric

teaching policy.[24]   I would like to suggest why
it is, historically, intrinsically plausible for
this to be the case.

It is not that many complaints of ob-
scurity are likely to have arisen during Jesus'
public ministry: the indications in surviving
tradition are that he was generally known to
have taught openly and clearly——too clearly for
his own safety. But that which was taught about
him after the Resurrection was not obviously
and publicly identical with what many could remember his having taught before the Crucifixion.
That undoubtedly constituted an important stra-
tegic problem both internally and externally.
Externally, how could Christian preachers establish credibility, especially with those who had
heard Jesus teach, given this apparent conflict
or at least discontinuity? Internally, how
could they account for the failure of the Jesus
followers to realize at the time what was really happening?

There are primarily two ways for early
Christians to tackle the problem of apparent
discontinuity: (a) to acknowledge that the discontinuity was really there, that a new teaching
was introduced after the resurrection of Jesus,
and find a way of explaining why (God's plan
changed; the disciples had not yet been ready
to understand; the shift of the aeons); or

(b) to claim that what looks discontinuous is
really not so at all (we were told but forgot
or misunderstood; that earlier teaching was
really an allegory of this later one; some of
us could see it all along but couldn't yet reveal it). Early Christianity used both ways of
handling the problem, and several varieties of
each. The tradition was accordingly laced with
conflicting tendencies of explanation.

One of the more interesting of the con-
tinuity-affirming strategies was the representation that the crucifixion and resurrection of
Jesus, however surprising they might have seemed
to some people at the time, had in fact been
revealed well before the event—in the scriptures, and even in the instructions of Jesus
himself. If this claim could be backed, it
would be a convenience to the credibility of
what must have seemed to many outsiders and insiders alike as a somewhat startling and
strangely unanticipated kerygmatic news. Scriptural arguments were the strongest. We have
certainly lost some of the important details
from the exegetical activities inspired by early Christian efforts to demonstrate that these
events were "in accordance with the Scriptures,"
but we can hardly doubt that considerable attention and ingenuity were concentrated on this
task. Early Christians found texts which,

interpreted in certain ways, seemed to show
that the key events of Christian beginnings had
indeed been prophetically anticipated in the
Scriptures, even required by them.

　　　Scripture was a powerful argument, but
it was also worthwhile to be able to show that
Jesus himself had known and taught the approaching crucifixion and resurrection, the necessity
of his suffering as prelude to his glorifica-
tion.　Eventually, the tradition came to contain
straightforward and overt predictions placed in
the mouth of Jesus (obviously the clearest and
most unequivocal as well as the simplest way of
representing the claim).　But, as is suggested
by the accounts of the behavior of the disciples
at the time of the crucifixion, and even at the
first news of the resurrection, it was difficult
to claim that the disciples had really been in
on the secret.　Hence, the apparently clear predictions by Jesus tended to attract brief explanations of why these predictions were somehow
not understood, or not remembered, or not made
known at the time—and sometimes with a mere
helpless attempt to record the fact that they
were at any rate *not* understood, even if it was
impossible to say why.　But there was another
means available for representing Jesus' fore-
warnings, a means already well developed and
reliable: tendentious *exegesis*.　The techniques

applied to Scripture could be applied to other
texts as well. If it was not altogether persuasive to claim that Jesus had plainly announced his suffering and triumph, it was certainly possible to argue that he did so obliquely and symbolically, investing these unexpected
revelations in the recesses of his well-known
parables, to be grasped by those who had ears
to hear.

        We have one set of evidences to support
clearly just such a contention: the texts dealing with the parabolic claim that this sign-
hungry and wicked generation will get no sign
but the Sign of Jonah. Whether or not Jesus
had actually spoken the brief parable of Johah's
Sign, he was understood to have done so by the
tradition, early in its development. What did
this parable mean? Matthew presents it baldly
in 16:1-4, where it seems intelligible. The
version preserved by Luke (11:29-32) elaborates
on the obvious explanation: the command to repentance given through Jonah was itself the
sign, and the analogous command given through
Jesus is all the proof this generation needs or
will get. Matthew's other version (12:38-42)
is like Luke's, except for the insertion of a
single verse that goes diametrically against
the whole thrust of the parable and shows how
the potential manipulability of parabolic dis-

course got exploited. Verse 40 thus interprets
the Sign of Jonah: "For as Jonah was three days
and three nights in the belly of the whale, so
will the Son of Man be three days and three
nights in the heart of the earth." This interpretation is, of course, entirely inconsistent
with the dominant claim of this very parable
that they do not deserve any special sign, do
not need one, and shall not have one. It is
also inconsistent with the way in which the
surrounding verses interpret the parable, as
referring to the preaching of repentance. But
it is consistent with the early Christian need
to demonstrate that Jesus predicted the passion
and resurrection.

No one, during Jesus' public ministry,
would thus have interpreted the parable of
Jonah's sign: the other versions give the normal and plausible drift and are surely representative of original understandings. But it cannot be denied that there is an interesting analogue between the restoration of Jonah and the
restoration of Jesus. The parable must be
twisted if it is to yield such a meaning, but
can be made to seem to do so. What have we
then? A demonstration that there was, buried
in the parables that had instructed the crowds,
a hidden teaching that pointed to what the
closest disciples eventually realized. From

the point of view represented by verse 40, and
that viewpoint alone, the parable is not the
lucid metaphor it had seemed to be, but a cryp-
tic message in need of special explication.
From that viewpoint, no one would have been
able to grasp the parables of Jesus truly without the assistance of special instruction. The
crowds would have seemed to see, would have
thought they had heard, but the most important
revelation of the parable would elude them.

Matthew 12:40 may be later than Mark,
but it shows a technique that is almost certain
to have been used on the parables earlier. The
motif of esoteric revelation was already present
in pre-Marcan tradition, in at least the form of
special post-resurrection instruction to the
disciples. One may even readily allow that it
was likely to be connected specifically with
the parabolic teaching before it came to Mark;
Matthew 12:40 provides textual evidence that it
eventually was so connected. Tradition would
know, however dimly and imprecisely, that for a
time, only a very few of the many persons who
had listened to the parables of Jesus—only the
closest disciples—were able to see in the parables dark and generally undetected hints about
the more dramatic and scandalous portions of
the saving and revealing career of Jesus. Let
us grant, then, that the theme of esoteric

revelation through parables was already present
to very early tradition. How shall we account
for the peculiar form it takes in the Gospel of
Mark? How did esoteric revelation in parables,
discovered only after Jesus' resurrection, become inflected to an esoteric teaching before
his crucifixion, implemented through a special
private explanation of parables that were intended to be an instrument of deliberate concealment?

III.   UNRIDDLING THE RIDDLES

Eduard Schweizer has proposed a most ingenious theory, neatly reversing some of the
traditional suppositions about the Gospel's
composition.[25] It was not Mark, Schweizer suggested, who established the esoteric explanation of parables to the disciples: that, he believes, was already accomplished by pre-Marcan
tradition. Mark's major contribution was to
demonstrate that it did not work. Thus,
Schweizer's sense of the history of the crucial
parts of Mark 4 is as follows: (a) Mark inherited the parable of the Sower, and the explanation, from the tradition, and the two were at
that point already linked by some earlier form
of verses 10 (the transition and question about
the parable) and 13a (surprise or reproof that

they do not understand the parable); (b) the
next stage of development—also pre-Marcan—
brought verse 10 into something more like its
present form and added the theory of esoteric
purposes found in 11-12: thus the essential
problem of the esoteric teaching from concealing parables was already there before Mark made
his own original and decisive contribution.
Keeping the sharp division of the Twelve from
the rest of the people, and also Jesus' special
attention to them (both of which would belong
to earlier tradition), Mark added 13b, Jesus'
reproof, so as to show that despite all their
special advantages, the closest disciples are
also among the blind who, hearing, do not hear.
The moral of the story—and the purpose of this
editorial maneuver—is, Schweizer suggests, that
the mystery of the Kingdom can be truly understood only through the way of discipleship, following the cross of Jesus. Mark had confronted
a problem created by the opposition of two traditional themes: on the one hand, revelation in
Jesus was too strong to be restrained, and must
break through; on the other hand, the mystery
of God's purposes is and was too deep to be
penetrated. The blindness of the disciples,
emphatically presented in the midst of special
teaching, is Mark's way of resolving this thematic difficulty. The cross was to be the way

by which God's purposes are revealed, openly and
unrestrainedly, through Jesus. All are called;
but only along the way of the cross is understanding possible. All are blind until then,
impenetrably.

According to this theory, the difficulties caused by the key esoteric-teaching verses,
10-13a and 34, are not Mark's responsibility.
They were part of his inherited material, not
part of his composition. They are therefore not
to be laid to the charge of Mark's reputation,
and Mark is left free to be creatively and pur-
posefully inventive. Theodore Weeden, respond-
ing enthusiastically to Schweizer's suggestions,
argues that these verses must be pre-Marcan and
not to be blamed on Mark:

> First, if 4:34...is Markan
> redaction, then Mark must have
> either been a very careless,
> inconsistent writer or very
> feebleminded thinker. For
> even a cursory reading of the
> Gospel shows that Jesus did
> not teach *only* in parables.
> Second, if 4:34 and 4:11-12
> are labeled as Markan redac-
> tional activity...Mark again
> betrays his literary and in-
> tellectual ineptitude.[26]

Weeden's language is perhaps stronger
than I would use, but the basic insight is quite
correct. If Mark had written these verses, he

would have come out seeming decidedly inept.
But, unfortunately for the Schweizer-Weeden protection of Mark's reputation, it seems to me
that we do not get him importantly off the hook
merely by claiming that Mark ineptly *retained*
these awkward and counterproductive verses rather than having ineptly composed them in the
first place. To be sure, Weeden acknowledges
that there is some madness here, and argues
that there is nevertheless method in it; and
after posing the crucial question, "then why did
Mark use material that sets itself in such diametric opposition to his own point of view?"[27]
he sets out to propose an answer. But aside
from the problem of whether the motive he postulates is either plausibly constructed or con-
vincingly argued, there remains the difficulty
that the materials are in diametric opposition.
The resulting inconsistency is not effectively
functional as it stands. Whichever was Mark's
own view, he has incorporated material quite
alien to it, and has managed the contradiction
not with a finesse that reveals a lesson but
with a benumbing baldness that leaves us either
bemused or scrambling to our own resources for
an explanatory subtlety that is painfully lack-
ing in the text.
        It seems to me quite clear that Schwei-
zer's account and Weeden's both, like

Marxsen's,[28] display admirable ingenuity but
cannot sustain Mark through the bottom-line test
of interpretive plausibility: imaginative historical replication. For if we suppose, hypo-
thetically, that Schweizer or any particular in-
terpreter is accurate; that the intentions which
he attributes to the author are the true ones;
that these were indeed the original motives, the
original program to be promoted, the message and
effect to be put across—then does it seem likely that the author would have chosen these words,
these phrasings, these tones and images and as-
sociations and configurations of story, as the
apt way to accomplish his ends? Interpreters
must develop theories to explain texts. But it
is not enough to concoct a theory that provides
a way of reading the text: it should provide a
way of *writing* it. A given text can occasion a
variety of apparently plausible theories about
what the author was doing; but one must then
ask whether a given theory of the author's purposes would plausibly have occasioned the text
as we have it. The theory of resurrectional
reference advanced by Matthew 12:40 makes its
own kind of interpretive sense, but it is not
credible to propose that Jesus would have used
the sign-denying parable of the Sign of Jonah
as a way of referring to his resurrection. In
the present case, this test seems to me to be

decisive.

Schweizer presumes that the rest of the
text was already essentially formed in its
present condition before Mark added the last
twist of 13b (how then will you know all the
parables?), and postulates that the twist itself was intended to discredit the disciples'
perspicacity and to point to Mark's conviction
that the mystery of the Kingdom can be understood only from the perspective of the way of
the cross, where all are equally called. The
main trouble with this interpretation[29] is that
it is cancelled by the movement of the text.
The disciples do not understand, and Jesus—
with a sudden change in tone—wonders how they
will manage to understand all parables if they
do not understand this one. But verse 34 as-
sures us that the problem was resolved by the
application of special esoteric teaching. Far
from humbling the disciples by leaving them un-
comprehending, or dramatically reducing the
distinction between insiders and outsiders, or
making all true understanding evidently dependent on the cross, Mark's final version implies
that right understanding of the mystery of the
Kingdom depends on Jesus' selective private explanations of parables, and in the given example it appears to have nothing whatever to do
with the cross. The disciples may be dull, but

they are graciously rescued from their dullness,
not by the way of the cross but by special tu-
torials. If Mark invented the question posed
in 13b, it can hardly have been with the hope
of reversing the evident meaning of all that
tidily follows in the rest of the chapter; and
if the disciples remain unenlightened enough to
stumble and misunderstand on the occasion of
later revelations, the text of Chapter Four
nevertheless establishes that they are safely
provided for where parables are concerned, and
that this apparently largely takes care of
giving them to understand the mystery of the
kingdom.

Had Mark had in mind what Schweizer and
Weeden have in mind, he would not have written
as he did. Whatever he received from tradition,
even if he felt reluctantly obliged to include
some of it willy-nilly, it is scarcely imaginable that Mark could have rested content with
including so much and adjusting so little had
he been pursuing the purposes attributed to him.
I further suggest that it is difficult to imagine that he would have written as he did, with
such a confused and confusing portrait of Jesus'
dispositions and decisions, if he had his writing under control in general, whatever aims it
may have been intended to serve.

There is one further difficulty in the

theories of Schweizer and Weeden. Not only do
they ultimately fail to rescue Mark from the
charge of clumsy redaction, but they also fail
to attend to the curious clumsiness which they
implicitly acknowledge to have infected the
earlier stages of tradition. Whether invented
by Mark or inherited by him, these peculiar
formulations of the problem of Esoteric Teaching remain importantly problematic. Why and
how were they composed, even if we may not be
able to determine precisely by whom? It is to
that investigation that we must turn before
attempting to locate Mark's role in the process,
in the hope of recovering a sense of the purposes that seem here to be so strongly blurred
and dislocated.

IV. THE COMPOSITION OF MARK 4

If we return to the peculiarities of
Chapter Four, we can sort out some of the stages
of development. Starting arbitrarily with the
parable of the Sower and its explanation, we
can readily concede that these two must have
been linked consistently from the time the latter came into being, and that this stage ante-
dated Mark.[30] The original linkage between them
needed no more than a simple transitional turn
that could modulate from parable to explanation,

such as "And they asked him about the parable.
And he said..." The parable's setting in a
public teaching is also undoubtedly early and
pre-Marcan, and the same is true of the explanation: both the overall Gospel tradition and the
internal indications in Mark's fourth chapter
suggest clearly that at some pre-Marcan stage,
this parable, its explanation, and some or all
of the succeeding parables were represented as
part of a continuous flow of public discourse
before the explanation was artificially and in-
completely separated from the parable by the
awkward privatizing twist of 10a (and the failure to provide the necessary subsequent modulation back into the public setting, where the
scene obviously ends). 33 is clearly part of
that earlier public framework. So, undoubtedly,
are the smaller parables that flow from 20 (the
end of the Sower explanation) to 33, which sums
up Jesus' instructing the crowd in such parables. (It is worth noting in passing that the
first of these smaller parables, that of the
lamp in 21-3, is provided with a sort of summary explanation—and that with or without the
explanatory words, the meaning is clearly supportive of the open revelatory intention of the
whole discourse, just as the summary in 33
would have it.)

    34b, on the contrary, offers an emphatic

thrust against the whole spirit and conduct of
the public discourse, as if trying to vitiate
what otherwise has been represented as effective, to privatize to the disciples what has
otherwise been shown as deliberately in the
public domain and possibly even to impute motives for parabolic discourse that are essentially opposite to the motives otherwise implied.
When and how would these touches have been added, so against the grain of the rest?   And
above all, *why*? The questions that apply here
apply *a fortiori* to the remainder, 10-13, with
their darker purposes and darker moods that
stand starkly at antipodes to the balance of
the chapter.   Be these Marcan inventions or traditional inheritances, what is their origin?
What motives went into their formation?   And
how could it ever have seemed anything but un-
intelligibly incoherent for these various pieces
to be put together in the same immediate context?

        If we dissect 10-13 along the lines of
its discernible parts, on the supposition that
they might not always have been thus joined, we
may find clues to their possibly independent ac-
cretions to this context. Verse 10 appears
composite: the question about the parable is so
apt to the transition into the subsequent explanation that it must be closely associated

with it as an early stage of traditional development; the move into a private context, however, "And when he was alone," is so out of
keeping with the main drift of this story of
public discourse that it must be late and artificially imposed. "Those who were with him" is
ambiguous, sounding (because awkward and unnecessary as a reference to the crowds) slightly more self-conscious than the earliest stage,
while the additional specification "with the
Twelve" reads like special pleading—plausibly,
this is a special addition to the general reference to the private audience, for the purpose
of making it unambiguously clear that this particular group is included. 11 and 12 break
more cleanly: 11 is a smoothly fluent statement
(though not exactly an answer to the question
posed in 10) that is not easily dismembered,
and 12 is obviously a quotation of or allusion
to Isaiah 6:9-10 and is thus also integral. 13
adverts to the question of 10, introducing two
questions of its own that are clearly related
but potentially separable both from each other
and from the explanation of the parable, which
then follows in 14.

On the surface, then, 10 appears to be
the most troubled and critically complex of
these four verses, while 11 and 12 together
seem the most solidly composed, and the least

tampered with by traditional patchwork. 12 in
particular, being a mere importation of Isaiah,
seems to be compositionally not in doubt. How
did this verse come into play as a member of
the Gospel tradition? That is, not just at
what stage, but in reference to what?

As a description of the response, or
non-response, of those to whom revelation was
presented, there are a few different points of
entry at which this would have made sense. It
could imaginably have been applied to those who
were exposed to the Scriptures but failed to
grasp their import and react accordingly. Or
it could (more plausibly) have been applied to
those who heard the preaching of Jesus and
failed to respond—this is, of course, the
sense of Luke's version of the parable of the
Sign of Jonah: Ninevah grasped the point and
repented, while the contemporaries of Jesus
failed to imitate that example and therefore
demonstrated both that they did not really hear
and see, and that they would not turn and be
forgiven. Or the quotation could have been
brought into play—or reused—to refer to a
slightly different gospel than the one here
preached by Jesus, namely, the gospel about his
own suffering, death, resurrection, and glory,
through which the early Church understood repentance and forgiveness to be supremely or

exclusively offered. In this case, it would be
like the interpolated version of the Sign of
Jonah found in Matthew: these salvific themes
were preached through coded parables, but the
hearers and seers did not in fact grasp the
deepest import and therefore did not respond
appropriately and win the salvation offered.

In any of these instance, the way the
Isaiah quotation is placed in Mark's fourth
chapter is a little out of phase with the rest.
It has nothing obvious to do with private instruction, either to need such a select audience for its setting or to motivate the formation of one. It also is clearly out of keeping
with the governing tendency of the overall public frame of the chapter, which evidently as-
sumes that Jesus' parabolic instruction was
meant to be, and mainly was, effective. It
seems obvious that verse 12 found its place in
the tradition as a comment on some relative unsuccess of Jesus' public teaching, the Isaian
quotation thus establishing that this was fore-
known or foreordained and not to be attributed
to any insufficiency in Jesus' proclamation.

There is no need to suppose that Mark
invented the application, since it not only is
in conflict with the main drift of the materials with which he has surrounded it, but is
readily eligible for at least two pre-Marcan

contexts. The same pattern of preaching and response that begat the optimistic picture given
in the main drift of the chapter (Jesus preached
helpful parables, adapted to the crowds' understanding, and they listened attentively) could
beget simultaneously another verdict in a less
optimistic temperament (yes, they listened: but
they didn't change their lives and thus missed
the whole point). And, of course, if what is
to be seen and heard is the inception of the
ultimate kerygma the message about Jesus' future career and role together with the presence
of the one through whom salvation is to be effected, then the bitter Isaian verdict might
well be applied from a post-Easter perspective
to all who had followed Jesus in earlier days.

But it is the business of verse 11 to
claim that it did not apply to all. "Those who
were about him with the Twelve" are exempted.
When, in the formation of tradition (for again,
this conjunction is likely to be pre-Marcan),
was 11 joined with 12? There is only one possible answer: it happened when it was perceived
that some inner circle was privy to ultimate
salvific secrets that had been present in the
teaching of Jesus but somehow hidden within
them.

The tradition is almost universally inclined to attest that the comportment of the

closest disciples, before, during, and immediately after the crucifixion of Jesus, did not
much distinguish them from any general incomprehension that might be attributed to the crowds
that heard Jesus. While it is possible that
the moment of their privilege might originally
have been located in some special instruction
given to them earlier, as the placement of 11
in Mark would have it, there are many reasons
to be dissatisfied with this way of situating
the saying. The overwhelming weight of positive
and negative evidence suggests that the statement formulated in Mark 4:11 originally sprang
from a post-resurrection context, as the closer
disciples reinterpreted the public career of
Jesus in the new way that is reflected in Matthew's Sign of Jonah and saw that their new
post-resurrection understanding was an esoteric
comprehension of what had been publicly offered.

I have chosen slightly evasive terms in
key places in the previous sentence, in order
to leave room for the possibility that the
early post-resurrection context was not only
the one in which this verse originated, but
even the locus of its reference. We read it
automatically as referring to the parables
preached by Jesus, and Matthew's version of the
Sign of Jonah comes conveniently to hand as an
illustration of the process of adaptation. But

Mark 4:11 does not say that everything is
preached in parables to the outsiders. If it
did, it would require some further interpretation, since up to that point—and generally in
the tradition preserved by the Synoptic gospels
—parables were preached to everyone, and did
not constitute a disadvantage: we would have to
understand "preached exclusively in obscure
parabolic form, by contrast with—" With what?
Not with direct explication, at least not according to verse 11. The explication does indeed follow after 13, but has not yet been
promised or referred to. The parables are con-
trasted with an access available to the insiders: "to you is given the mystery" (*humin
dedotai to mysterion*). *Parables* has here evidently lost its previous sense of illuninating
illustration and has somehow come to mean *riddles*.

    If verse 11 said that everything is
preached in parables to outsiders, it would require some further interpretation. But it does
not say this. It says that to those outside,
by contrast with those to whom the mystery is
given, "all things *happen* in parables" (*en
parabolais ta panta ginetai*). I suggest that
the reference is not to the characteristic
preaching so much as to the decisive *events* of
Jesus' public career. The outsider sees only

the disappointing fizzle of the promising movement of liberation, the embarrassing humilia-
tion of the convicted pretender, the shocking
and definitive ignominy of his rough public ex-
ecution. The insider, once the resurrection
light dawns, sees that these are not direct
ordinary signs of a discouraging truth but riddles, parables, to which they now have the key.
To them is imparted the mystery of the Kingdom;
to others, only the parable itself is visible—
only the riddle without the answer, the unusual
metaphor without the illuminating insight that
makes it fall into place and gives one to know
what it is intended to reveal. I suggest that
the verse that eventually found its way into
the public teaching context of Mark's fourth
chapter originated in that very different setting and was aimed at this very different meaning.

Verse 11 thus may have originated in
early post-resurrection circles, with reference
not to the earlier teaching of Jesus but to the
matters that most preoccupied his followers in
those critical days. The adaptation of the
Isaian verse 12 to Christian purpose may possibly have occurred then too, and might have been
joined to 11 readily (though it may have arisen
independently, and possibly slightly earlier).
But here some further distinction must be made.

Verse 12 is clearly derivative of Isaiah 6:9-10,
but there were three possible ways for it to be
derived. One was to cite the Hebrew text to
Isaiah. Another was to cite the Greek translation of that text. The third was to cite the
Aramaic version of it, the Targum. Mark's 4:11
is not a direct rendition of any of these. Which
of them lies originally behind this citation of
Isaiah for Christian purposes?

The question is potentially important,
because the three different significantly. Observe:

> Hebrew: And he said, "Go, and say
> to this people: 'Hear and hear, but
> do not understand; see and see, but
> do not perceive.' Make the heart of
> this people fat, and shut their eyes;
> lest they see with their eyes, and
> hear with their ears, and understand
> with their hearts, and turn and be
> healed."

> Greek: And he said, "Go, and say to
> this people, 'Hearing, you shall hear,
> and you shall not understand; and
> seeing, you shall not see, and you
> shall not perceive. For the heart
> of this people has become fat, and
> with their ears they hear dully, and
> they have closed their eyes, lest
> they should see with their eyes and
> hear with their ears and understand
> with their heart, and turn, and I
> heal them."

> Aramaic: And he said, "Go and speak

> to this people, who hear indeed
> but do not understand, and see
> indeed but do not know. Gross
> is the mind of this people, and
> its ears has it made heavy, and
> its eyes has it blinded, lest
> they should see with their eyes
> and with their ears should hear
> and with their minds should
> understand, and repent and ob-
> tain forgiveness."[31]

The differences are slight in wording, but
powerful in implication. The Hebrew text has
God charge Isaiah with the task of taunting the
people and making them unresponsive at the same
time, so as to prevent their understanding and
salvation. The LXX softens this dreadful instruction by changing the taunt to a prediction
and assigning the responsibility for their dull
rejection of the way of healing to themselves
rather than to Isaiah's carrying out of God's
orders. The Targum takes the Hebrew original
to a still gentler form, in which God seems to
be sending Isaiah on an errand of mercy, but
with the sad awareness that they have closed
themselves off from response and forgiveness.
The shift in language is minor; the shift in
theological implication is enormous.

The ultimate source behind Mark 4:12
might be any of the three. If this passage was
appropriated early in the Christian tradition,
which is highly probable, the likelihood is

against the Greek version. The Hebrew original
may be the source; but there is a better case
to be made for the Targum as the immediate occasion, the most decisive linguistic evidence
being the final words: Hebrew and Greek speak
of healing, while Mark 4:11 agrees with the
Aramaic text in speaking rather of forgiveness.
This and other linguistic evidences, for which
the reader may consult Matthew Black's discussion of this passage,[32] are supported by general plausibility, for the Targum's Aramaic rendition was undoubtedly heard in the synagogues
of Palestine, and it would have been primarily
in Aramaic that the quotation would have circulated in early Christian circles; but more to
the point, the deliberate adjustments which the
Targum makes upon the Hebrew text obviously
render it more theologically intelligible and
homiletically useful.[33] It would not much have
served either Judaic or Jewish-Christian purposes to promote the thought that God calculatedly impeded salvation, either in ancient or
in modern times. It would be decidedly advan-
tageous to both, and surely more consonant with
the ways in which the Gospels represent what
actually happened, to suggest rather than the
people are self-blinded and dull of heart,
themselves perversely resisting the chance to
be forgiven. The odds are strongly in favor of

the more benevolent Targum adaptation being the
ultimate, even if not the immediate, source of
Mark 4:12.

A Targumic version of this passage would
have fit suitably into any context from John
the Baptist onward. After all, it describes
the perennial problem. No decisive *Sitz im
Leben* can be determined for it. Indeed, it is
likely to have been a favorite of any impatient
or disappointed preacher from the time of its
composition until the fading of colloquial
Aramaic. The likelihood is that it was in general circulation (especially in the prosely-
tizing apocalyptic circles with which early
Christianity was associated) and would readily,
if casually, be attracted to supplement Mark 4:
11, with its scoff at the outsiders who cannot
penetrate the parables, as soon as that saying
entered the field.

Which brings us to another necessary distinction. It is not unlikely that in early
post-resurrection days, a reflection upon the
difference between those to whom it has been
given to know the mystery and those who see
only riddles where the former see revelation
might have remembered in a benevolent spirit
the regretful observation of the Isaiah Targum
that (through their own fault) most people see
but do not understand. Such a combination

might well be the ultimate *Vorlage* of Mark 4:11-
12. But that is not what Mark gives us. His
text is not the Targum's gentle exasperation.
That would explain the relative failure of the
parables in question by the fact that some people simply do not have ears to hear, essentially because of their hardheartedness. What Mark
presents is bent back toward the darker meaning
of the original Hebrew Isaiah: what happens is
happening in parables *so that* those who are
outside may be left in the dark and excluded
from repentence and forgiveness. In the context in which Mark presents it, the implication
is even worse: Jesus is teaching in parables as
a strategy of deliberate obfuscation in order
to prevent the outsiders from seeing, repenting,
and being forgiven. Whether we take the combination of the actual Marcan verses 4:11-12 in
their received context, as a plan enacted by
Jesus in his teaching, or suppose them to have
been originally applied to Jesus' later career,
referring to God's intent to disguise the meaning of saving events so that some might be excluded from salvation, the effect is nasty.
The revelational technique is both pointlessly
self-defeating and dishonestly misleading. Any
attempts to evade this judgment on Mark's working of 4:12 are nothing but attempts to plead
for what Mark *meant* to say. What he actually

succeeded in saying is unequivocal, and is, as
Matthew Black has put it, a "grim adaptation"[34]
which wrenches the verse out of whatever might
remain of its kinder Targumic alternative or of
its partial compatibility with the sense of benevolent revelation that prevails in both general early Christian received tradition and in
the rest of Mark's fourth chapter. The effect
is horrendous, and requires an explanation.

       Where, in the history of forms and redac-
tions, does this curiosity fit? Where might it
make procedural sense? If the latter is taken
to mean tenable theological sense, then the answer is plain: nowhere, never. It is a theological outrage, whatever its trajectory of origin. If, on the other hand, we ask when or
where or in what circumstances it might have
been thought temporarily useful and satisfactory,
then the answer must again be indefinite. If
such a proposition can be believed at all, it
can be believed anywhere, anytime. Desperate
anger at the failures of Isaiah's mission seems
to have occasioned its near-equivalent originally; similar conditions may induce the theologically unreflective to employ it ever after.
If you are willing to blame either God or his
elected deputy for a policy of deliberate misleading opacity in revelation, not only resulting in, but *for the purpose of,* preventing re-

pentance and forgiveness, then you can apply
this to Isaiah, or Elijah, or John the Baptist,
or the preaching of Jesus, or the Crucifixion—
or the establishment of the Papacy, or the Ref-
ormation, or the emergence of contemporary Biblical criticism. It is a wild card, and can be
played on any trick. Any theological game that
permits it is not worth playing. Historically,
however, it might emerge anywhere. The question
at hand is therefore its emergence in Mark 4:11-
12, and the wording of the question is not so
much Whence? as Why?

Whether the redactional development that
placed these verses in this context is to be attributed to Mark or to antecedent tradition,
there could have been no motivation whatsoever
for adducing the content of verses 11-12 to the
scene of the public parabolic teaching until
there arose a misgiving about whether the parables were really illustrations or riddles. I
do not think that the evidence suggests that
this happened during Jesus' public ministry.
Received tradition does not indicate that they
were regarded as riddles by the crowds. We do
not have notice of rumors or dissatisfied puz-
zlement, or accusations of frustrating incompre-
hensibility. Recent scholars of the parables
have drawn to our attention that they can be
read as paradoxical, disorienting, unsettlingly

mysterious. I grant that this is so, given
certain ways of reading. Certainly some of the
extant parables are no longer quite intelligible, even if they originally had a context that
made them lucid. It is even imaginable that
Jesus designed some of them to be baffling.
But if so, the major body of traditional lore
has missed the intent. Where it might show the
crowd's confusion, it suggests the opposite. The
global picture gives us the impression of successful teaching and learning through parables.
If anyone should wish to adduce Mark 4:11-12 as
wiser evidence to the contrary, I submit that
these verses merely claim that the overall received tradition of successful public parabolic
teaching is illusory, and simultaneously claim
that it was intended to be so for essentially
malevolent purposes. Weigh the probabilities.
In my own judgment, the verisimilitude lies
clearly with the general tradition and decisive-
ly against the interpretation given by Mark 4:
11-12, as well as firmly against the hypothesis
that Jesus used an alternative version of esoteric teaching (parables as disruptive koans)
that has been brutally misunderstood in these
verses. It is not sufficiently credible to
propose that Mark 4:11-12 is only an unfortu-
nate misformulation of an essential truth,
blissfully unknown to those who passed on the

general lore and wretchedly bungled by those
who managed to insert it here against the tide
of the context. Even the principle of clumsiness has its limits.

Mark 4:11-12 entered the picture of parabolic discourse only when there arose some
doubt about whether the parables were illustrations or riddles. Overwhelmingly, it seems to
me, that points to the moment of post-resurrection reinterpretation. More exactly, I suggest
that it points to the complex of moments of
realization in which the followers of Jesus (a)
recognized that the apparent failure, defeat,
punishment, and death of Jesus, the key events
of early Christian kerygma, were essentially
parables of revelation, their significance
grasped by the initiate but opaque to the others (quite plausibly using the term "parables"
to refer to this phenomenon, with one of its
available connotations of "riddles" rather than
"illustrative tales"); (b) noticed that the illustrative parables of Jesus' preaching could
be read as secret revelations of those later
events together with their revelational meanings; and (c) recognized that in fact virtually
no one—perhaps no one at all—had noticed at
the time what any of these spoken or enacted
parables might mean when read in a different
way. Out of this complex of realizations might

readily arise internally—not as a castigation
of the principals by their critics, but in their
own joyful if chagrined self-criticism—the tradition of representing the closest disciples as
unhappily dim and dumbheaded, having been given
what eventually was taken as clear revelation
and yet, despite their closeness to the Master,
unable to grasp its import. The dullest of the
universally dull: a self-judgment that arises
naturally and spontaneously from those who finally see, and find themselves wonderfully privileged as a result. Outside critics are likely
to be kinder. The principals can more readily
afford spreading this forgiven slander against
themselves. Others, later, may no longer understand the context in which the criticism was
made, or remember the identity of the critics;
and a vague tradition of this sort easily fer-
ments into a narrative that merely tries to re-
count what took place, what failed to take
place, what judgments were placed upon it all
by some authoritative voices.

A similar ferment, arising from a different track, makes heroes of those who finally
understood. They have not taken credit for the
revelation, as if it had been their discernment:
on the contrary, it arrived in despite of their
incapacities. Somehow, mysteriously, unto them
it was given to know the mystery, while it re-

mains still an unsolved riddle to the outsiders, despite their experience of the revealing source. From this point in tradition, with the inner circle both vilified (at their own insistence) and celebrated for their privilege (by their own gratitude and that of those who follow them), it is not difficult to understand how the materials that flowed to Mark through the multiplicity of ordinarily clumsy tellers of tales might converge in a seeming paradox of dull-witted disciples who are specially illuminated, a paradox that could not be readily resolved by a similarly clumsy, though imaginative and inventive,redactor.

They might, of course, have converged before Mark. They probably did. Several such conflicting views were in undiscriminating circulation. It is not unlikely that the conflict between the summary of effective parabolic teaching in 4:33 (arising from the time of Jesus' preaching) and the darker hints of riddle and exegesis in 4:34 (arising originally from post-resurrection insight) came to him in some form simultaneously, and that, unwilling or unable to choose, he passed them both on to his successors. I suppose that many such clumsy non-resolutions to the problems of the tradition took place well before Mark came on the scene, and presented themselves similarly,

though probably in other forms, to Matthew and
Luke. Mark is likely to be only one version of
many which the later evangelists encountered,
if indeed they were later than he. But how did
they converge on Mark? And what did he do with
them?

Mark 4:11-12 is set conspicuously as the
introduction of the explanation of the parable
of the Sower. But it is not attuned to that
particularization. Like the summary dark verse
4:34, the references are to the plural, to the
general question of parables, not to the specific instance of the one just inquired about.
Verse 10, where the disciples raise the question, has strong textual and logical support
for a plural reading as well: they inquired
about the parables. Thus far, the fallout of
tradition makes historical sense. An issue was
raised about the parables in general (perhaps
first the parables of historical event, then by
analogy those of Jesus' discourses). When the
tellers of tradition reflected on the interpretation of parables, they remembered two things
which they did not manage fully to reconcile or
sort out. On the one hand, Jesus instructed
the crowds in parables, according to their capacity, and seemed to have done so with considerable success. On the other hand, there were
hidden meanings in the parables of Jesus which

the inner circle eventually managed to understand not through their own insight (for they
are rather remembered as being surprisingly
dull) but through extraordinary privilege. According to this latter pattern of remembrance,
a general question about parables could be met
by a routine reference to the Isaiah Targum:
theoretically, anyone might have understood at
the time (since the meanings were really there),
but everyone failed to do so because of the
dullness of their ears, the grossness of their
minds. Even the closest disciples, perhaps the
dimmest of all, failed to grasp the meaning,
and were not infrequently berated by Jesus accordingly.

      At this stage of development, the per-
spective was probably still post-resurrectional.
It was at that stage that it was given unto the
closest disciples to understand the mystery of
the Kingdom, while to those outside, everything
occurs in parabolic riddles. I should think it
likely that it would be shortly thereafter that
the application of the Isaiah Targum would have
soured toward the crueller original text in
some circles, under the pressure of resistance
to the early missionary attempt to explicate
the acted-out parables of Jesus' last days (and
possibly his spoken parables as well), since
the energies of exasperation within Mark's

version of the text are far more appropriate to
that critical time than to the earlier moments,
in which the division between inside and outside understanding was not so clear, and the
situation did not yet so clearly entail a last
chance to arrive at an insight that for the majority was not there, and was not readily
forthcoming, and was disastrous not to achieve.
Matthew's version of this quotation (13:14-15)
goes back to the LXX, with its softening of the
Hebrew text; Luke truncates the quotation into
a brief paraphrased tag (8:10) that might come
ultimately from any of the three Isaian sources
but has in any event discarded important difficulties in the act of abbreviation. Mark alone
carries the harsher message, which may be harsher because of his own intervention, or because
some other teller had thus shaped it before him.
We probably cannot know which.

Originally, it appears that the general
statement about the parables in Mark 4:11-12
was introduced by an equally general question.
The best texts of Mark say that the disciples
asked him about the parables, plural. The
question eventually seems unambiguous, since
Jesus eventually seems to answer by explaining
the parable of the Sower; but in its place the
ambiguity is there. It did not necessarily
mean that they asked how to understand the

parables, and Matthew's version takes the ambiguity in the other direction by having them
ask, "Why do you speak to them in parables"
(13:10). I.e., the introductory question was
about the general practice, not the particular
parable just uttered. Mark 4:11-12 responds
likewise to a general question, and is much
better suited to a question about the practice
than one about specific meanings. Again, the
issue of parabolic preaching in general is not
likely to arise in any important way out of the
kind of experience represented in Mark 3 and in
the main body of 4. Verse 10 has the air of a
straight-man's or interviewer's question, designed to draw out the pre-existing answer of
11—a sort of dramatic catechism, for which the
question was composed last. The choice of in-
terviewers is apt: it is these closer disciples
for whom the strategy of parabolic teaching
first became a question, because it was they
who first learned to read them as if they were
riddles and, by doing so, saw the important distinction between those outside and those who
are privileged to understand. (Mark's strange
"those who were with him, with the Twelve" is
undoubtedly a conciliating conflation of two
versions, one of which, as in Matthew and Luke,
spoke of the disciples, another of which, like
John 6:67, insisted on specifying the Twelve.)

It is fitting that the statement of their privilege is not given as news about what *will* happen but mere acknowledgement of what *is* happening, as if that is not really news at all—just as it is fitting that Matthew has them ask why Jesus speaks in parables to "them," not to "us." This part of Mark 4:10, like 4:11-12, thus seems to retain the logic of a later, post-resurrectional, context, and to be inserted here, in a public teaching in parables, rather artificially, even apart from the artificiality of the abrupt move into privacy at the beginning of the verse. But that privatizing move now makes sense in the history of composition, even if it interrupts the overall flow of the chapter. For since 11 is obviously addressed to a more private and select audience (and *a fortiori* if it came to Mark already introduced by a version of 10 that specified a private audience, which is not improbable although not required), then the insertion of these verses here requires a modulation out of the public frame established earlier in the chapter. It is done in a perfunctory way, without any attention to motive or reason, but the minimum shift has been accomplished.

It is only in verse 13 that the discussion moves from the general question of parables (and probably of their existence rather than their meaning) to a specific attention to

the parable of the Sower. "And he said to them,
'Do you not understand this parable?'" But
that has not really been in question: they have
not asked about it and he has not been speaking
about it. "How then will you understand all
the parables?" Then follows the explanation of
the Sower. But the composition of 13 is as odd
as an introduction to the explanation as it is
as a conclusion to 10-12. A specific exegesis
of this parable will not automatically empower
them to understand the others, especially given
the banal exegesis that is now offered. If
they need this explanation, how indeed will they
understand all the parables? If they get this
explanation, how will that resolve their problem with *all* the parables? The fact that the
question of 13b is posed and not specifically
answered makes its rhetorical implication seem
to be "no way," which makes sense in terms of
the tradition of the disciples' dull-mindedness,
but abruptly gutters the sense of secure and
achieved privilege offered in verse 11. We
have to wait for verse 34b to have the matter
fully clarified: "privately to his own disciples
he explained everything." It is that one verse
that fully establishes the theme of an esoteric
teaching on the parables, by giving a generalizing interpretation of the relationship between
the explanation of the Sower and the general

themes of parabolic teaching and privileged
understanding that had been inserted just before it.[35]

Such an interpretation is probably the
reason for the insertion of 10-12 in the first
place, even if the inserted verses do not themselves carry it in even their present form.
Not only Mark himself, but his recent predecessors as well, had found in tradition an already
established representation that Jesus privately
explained parables to the disciples. Matthew
provides a striking non-Marcan instance in
which Jesus and his disciples retire into the
house after a discourse in parables, whereupon
the disciples ask for, and receive (without hes-
itation or complaint on Jesus' part, as if this
is routine), an explanation of the parable of
the darnel in the field (13:36-43). Since this
explanation concludes with "He who has ears,
let him hear," and then launches Jesus into further unexplained parables, it is plausible that
it too was originally given as part of public
discourse rather than privately; but be that as
it may, its extant form shows that the combination of public parable and private explanation
was Mark's inheritance, not his invention. An
earlier stage of tradition had already begun,
however randomly and inconsistently, to divide
received parable from received explanation in

just this way. And if it had happened to the
darnel in the field, why not the Sower? Being
the most conspicuous example of the parable/
explanation pattern now extant, this was the
most clearly eligible for re-editing in conform-
ity with the supposition that somehow the parables were impenetrable, yet somehow the close
disciples broke the code. That supposition
probably owed something to the disciples' post-
resurrection reinterpretation of events as parabolic, something to the subsequent reinterpretation of Jesus' spoken parables, and something
to the general theory thence derived, formulated
in Mark 4:11-12 and parallels. The mutual at-
traction of these related elements makes it nat-
ural that a creative redactor might transpose
these latter verses from the place he found
them (a post-resurrection setting? or already
retrojected into a private audience after a general public teaching in parables?) and resettle
them in the narrow isthmus between the Sower
and the explanation—especially if the latter
was already redefined as a private communication.
Some form of Mark 4:10 may accordingly have been
in place before some form of 11-12 was introduced to that location, and indeed the singular
variant *parable*, attested in different ways in
several ancient witnesses to 4:10, may represent
the original state of the private version, the

plural being then either a correction assimi-
lating 10 to 11-12 or an accurate restoration
of what had originally preceded 11 in an earlier context. At any rate, the insertion of 11-
12 changed the focus enough to warrant an explicit shift back to the specific question of
the Sower parable; hence the functional, if
rather abrupt, question of 13a: "Do you not
understand this parable?"

That still leaves one piece of redaction
to be accounted for, the question posed in 13b,
which is even more abruptly discontinuous with
11-12 than 13a had been: "How then will you
understand all the parables?" What was the motive for the composition of this question,
which is so out of keeping with its immediate
environment? I suggest two possible solutions,
the second of which is compatible with the
first, and necessary for its completion.

On the one hand, this may be a relic of
an earlier state of the 11-12 theory of parables. It might originally have been a harmless
rhetorical question followed by a resolving answer—i.e., "Unto you it is given to understand,
but to the rest all remains only in parables;
and how then will you know all the parables?
This is how:..." The answer eventually took
the form of 34b, the practice of private explanation, whatever it might originally have

been. (Cf. Luke 24:45, where the risen Jesus
opens their understanding to understand the
scriptures rightly, in contrast with 24:47,
where he explains the individual texts.) But
if this had been the case, it would not account
for the retention of 13b, divorced from its
general answer and set in a context that changes
its thrust to exasperation. Allowing for a lit-
tel clumsiness, a partial accounting can be
given by considering the alternative possibility:

Suppose, with Schweizer, that 13b is in
fact the culminating redactional touch in this
passage. If we also suppose, with Schweizer,
that all the rest of the surrounding matter was
already in place before Mark came to it, then
it is difficult to find a completely satisfying
explanation for its invention. 13b offers too
little to dislodge the reassurances already
built into 10-11 (which is what Schweizer pro-
poses it is intended to do), and is too oddly
contrary to its surroundings in both tone and
implication to be a mere routine smoothing-out
of the rough hoints of traditional accumulation.
Mark might have settled for moving back to the
particular question of the Sower parable from
the general theory of special revelation and
riddling concealment, just as directly, simply,
and abruptly as he had gone from the parable
irself to the general theory. 13a would have

sufficed without the unhelpful and interrupting
13b. But it is not incredible that, having returned to the particular by Jesus' sudden reference to their incomprehension of the Sower
(which Mark supposes or remembers was the implication of the ambiguous question of verse 10),
Mark is triggered into a favorite reflex. They
do not understand this parable, yet they are
scheduled to understand all parables, as the inserted verse 11 has just claimed, however
strangely. The obvious question is *how?*—and
the momentary dilemma might well awaken Mark's
sense of the tradition's representation of the
disciples as unaccountably and vexingly opaque.
Luke has the resurrected Jesus berate Cleopas
and his companion for their failure to grasp
the secrets of scripture, including his suffering and glory (24:25-26); Mark likes to concen-
trate on their analogous failure to understand
pre-crucifixion revelations, and the present instance gives him his first chance to introduce
this motif, and to have Jesus chide them even
as he resolves the problem, as he will do again
in 4:40 (cf. 38-39), 7:18 (cf. 19-23), 8:33 (cf.
34-38), 9:19 (cf. 28-29). 7:18 shows Mark's
readiness to use this kind of response with respect to their incomprehension about a specific
parable: "And he said to them, 'Then are you also
without understanding? Do you not see that what-

ever goes into a man from outside cannot defile
him...?'" That example neatly parallels 4:13
in its tone, and 13a in its content, while the
generalizing of 13b is probably simply an extension of the recent generalizing of 11, and
the contrast between them in implication conveniently further motivates the tone of exasperation in 13b. Having indulged himself thus in
a favorite motif, probably without noticing the
incongruity of this instance, he characteristically lets it drop and goes calmly onward to the
established business of helpful exegesis, without troubling to adjust the inherited Sower explanation to fit these changed and more dramatic
conditions.

                    V.   THEORY ONCE MORE

        Why did the agents of the Synoptic tradi-
tion make these changes—the privatization of
exegesis of the Sower and other parables, and
the displacement of the general theory of riddling concealment and revelation? The parable
and its explanation might have been left as they
had probably been found, directly joined in the
flow of public discourse, and the remarks about
the special communication of the mystery of the
Kingdom might have found (or remained in) a
more convenient and convincing place, in a pri-

vate aside after a public parabolic session, or
even in a post-resurrection explanation. The
earlier states of the tradition[36] were undoubtedly, in these instances, somewhat less unsatisfactory. Why were they tampered with?

I suggest that it was because the drift
of tradition had created a puzzling problem
which creative participants perceived, and that
the resolution which most readily suggested itself was sufficiently easy and superficially
satisfying that it obscured the more difficult
but accurate solution, and inspired redactional
adjustments that obscured it even further. What
the Synoptic predecessors could see in the theory of esoteric parabolical revelation as it lay
before them in tradition was only that there was
a discrepancy between what the closest disciples
grasped by privileged aid and what the crowds
had learned. The former saw the mystery of the
Kingdom; the latter saw but yet did not see.
But what they found in the tradition was apparently not clear about the character or the content of this privileged understanding, only
about the general fact—about as much as could
be summed up in a prior version of Mark 4:11-12.
Presumably, much of the special revelation
through parables had already been transposed into overt statement, as Matthew 12:40 became an
announcement by Jesus, the stage of parable

interpretation having quietly dropped out of the
tradition; or as Mark himself insists on the explicit plainness of Jesus' predictions of the
Passion (which were also undoubtedly esoteric
explanations originally), leaving him unable to
account for the disciples' failure to understand
them. It was a commonplace of tradition that
Jesus characteristically addressed the crowds in
parables, and it was another commonplace of tradition that the disciples came to know secrets
of the parables that were hidden from the crowds.
In the matter at his disposal, the creative teller of tales could see the parables of Jesus and
some explanatory non-parabolic passages. He did
not know that the important esoteric explications
were no longer presented as such by the tradition, which had transformed them to Dominical
statements. I suggest that the decisive creative contribution was to fabricate the most economical theory and adjustment allowed by the
material at hand: the parables were left to be
what they had always been, the public teaching
of Jesus—but the explanations, although they
had come to tradition as part of that same public teaching, were aligned with that non-parabolic private illumination which tradition
spoke of so darkly. Hence the redactor constructed his main distribution of parabolic and
explanatory material accordingly (though not
consistently), finding ways of getting the dis-

ciples aside for explanations and coloring the
whole with a theory of esoteric revelation that
had originally been concerned with a less banal
form of exegesis, no longer directly reflected
in the extant explanatory material.

Was he not puzzled to discover that the
first result was to move the mountain of a se-
cretly-delivered mystery of the Kingdom, only to
bring forth the relatively *ridiculus mus* of the
explanation of the Sower parable? Not if we
may judge from Mark's own achievements in the
shaping of stories—or from the byproducts of
his version of this one: an unacceptable and
strangely vexing opacity on the part of the disciples, who now must ask for fairly obvious explanations and be chided; and a solemn and
ominous plan of esoteric disclosure, unjust and
incongruous as a plan and unconvincingly anti-
climatic as an accomplishment. Likely enough,
Mark was satisfied that the explanations of the
parabolical items, however ordinary they may
have seemed, somehow lifted the veil of the
mystery of the Kingdom. His picture of the
disciples' helpless lack of comprehension is
arresting and memorable, even if inexplicable;
his sketch of the dark strategy of Jesus is
thrillingly impressive, however unbecoming.
Such effects may well have been enough to com-
mend these touches to Mark, whatever awkwardness
others might eventually see in their psychologi-

cal and theological implications, or in their
dubious alignment with other of Mark's own rep-
resentations. Once more, a little facility in
story-telling is a dangerous thing. It has put
a lamp under a bushel, and subverted the divine
justice by yet another mystification.

CHAPTER FIVE

CONCLUSION

What should we expect to find in a Synoptic Gospel? It is perhaps better to try not to answer the question. The answers that have conventionally been given in successive waves of Gospel criticism have been misled and misleading. No, we should not expect direct communications from the Holy Spirit, nor the findings of the earliest Christian historical heritage commission—nor a fabric woven on the warp of intent proclamation and the woof of self-articulating community needs. We still do not understand what a Gospel was. The Gospel form despite all attempts to explain it by analogy with this or that pre-Christian literary mode, or to derive it from putative laws of traditional development, remains a mysterious Christian invention. It was a novelty that was not inevitable. We do not yet have a sound way of determining how it was meant to be read. We do not yet know what we should expect to find in a

Synoptic Gospel, or why.

     This book has nevertheless proposed a
partial answer to the question, despite the potential folly of doing so. I make no claim to
understand what Gospels were quite supposed to
be, and therefore do not suggest what they are
meant to be read as. Along those critical lines,
I must settle for acknowledging that the ways
that have been proposed for resolving that problem, the claims that the Gospels are meant to be
read as God's oracles, or allegories of the
eschaton, or biographical studies of Jesus, or
proclamations of Jesus' risen Lordship, simply
do not strike me as persuasive. I do not think
that the heart of this unusual literary mystery
has been plucked out. I have no novel solution
to offer in place of the various imaginative but
ultimately unsatisfactory solutions which have
been proposed.

     But I have nevertheless tried to offer a
partial answer, not to the question about what
we should expect to find that a Synoptic Gospel
offers to be seen as, but to another dimension
of the question of what we should expect to find
in one. We should expect to find the leaven of
ordinary clumsiness, the same sort of ordinary
clumsiness that we see all around us in modern
oral tradition and that we have no good reason
to suppose the Synoptic tradition would have

been spared. And accordingly, we should expect
to find homely awkwardness, incoherence, occasional opacity, varying degrees of sheer misunderstanding: the usual. We should not expect
to find great editorial skill, or exacting
stylistic control, or an inheritance of stories
that are either rigorously determined or miraculously consistent and regular. We should expect to find something rather like what Mark offers.

What he offers is not egregiously bad
(although it is sometimes utterly unsuccessful)
nor memorably good (although it sometimes suc-
ceeds nicely). What comes through his redactional efforts and through the antecedent obscure history of traditional development is what
one might have expected *a priori* if not distracted by prepossessions. There is a certain
rough basic competence in the telling of tales
and in the crude linkages by which they are organized together, although in both cases the
Gospel seems to show evident dependence on the
immediate impact and organizational advantages
of the major events themselves. There is an
uneven performance in the setting-forth of the
material, which is presented in stumbling and
awkward narratives, full of anticlimaxes in the
ordering of units, unaccountable variations in
the texture of detail, laconic abbreviations

intermixed with inefficient ramblings, and ordinary bumblings of every sort. There is no
sign of particularly great story-telling distinction either in the final redactor or in the
cumulative effect of antecedent tradition.
There is an air of a great ordinariness with
which these extraordinary events were understood, told, retold, related to one another, co-
ordinated in ambitious thematic and interpreta-
tive ways that embrace contradictions, trip occasionally over their own creative boldness,
manage sometimes bravely and sometimes not at
all. This is an ordinariness capable of occasional felicity and occasional disaster; and
there are accordingly occasional felicities,
and occasional disasters, to be found within
the borders of the Gospel of Mark, some of them
undoubtedly compiled and confected through the
accumulating efforts of many previous tellers,
before Mark ever entered the picture. We find
a mirror of the human condition.

     I suggest that there are mainly three
lessons to be learned from approaching the Synoptic tradition in general, or the Gospel of
Mark in particular, in this way. The first lesson is the obvious one: the leaven of clumsiness
is manifestly operative, on various scales and
in varying degrees, throughout the received
material. Gospels were not privileged to

escape the weaknesses that are capable of producing a range of effects all the way from mildly awkward turns of phrase to massive blunders
that ruin the intelligibility or force of tales
that even the author believes to be important.

The second lesson follows from the first:
if the leaven of clumsiness is at work, then in
order to deal with these texts adequately—in
order to see what is going on and to be able to
account for it intelligibly—criticism must be
ready to make sense not by straining for a hidden purposefulness but by discerning the linea-
ments of careless inadvertence, failed strategies, distracted attention, sheer misunderstanding, and the like.

The third lesson has to do with the principle of clumsiness only from a certain perspective. It is obvious that the Gospel of Mark
shares with its antecedent tradition a great
preoccupation with the good news that arises
out of or is otherwise connected with the things
that Jesus did and said, and that the whole is
conditioned in important ways by the influence
of what the apostles subsequently did and said.
But if we hold either Mark or his tradition to
the responsibility of pursuing the transmission
of stories with an unwavering singlemindedness
of evangelical purpose, then we must judge them
both clumsy in this respect, for that is not the

way the stories come out: they have other interests, allow their attnetion to wander, occasionally enjoy the unevangelical fun of a lively
tale.   Some sort of clumsiness must be involved
here.   It may be in the tradition's, or the
redactor's, original performance, which surely
fails to carry out the work of proclaiming with
proper unswerving attention and careful technique.   But I do not impute this to Mark or his
predecessors as clumsiness, since I do not think
them obliged to follow such an austere and one-
sided program.   In this case, as this book has
tried to argue throughout, the operative clumsiness lies rather with modern critical expectation with their myths of evangelical form and
redaction criticism.   Beware their leaven.

NOTES

[1] Literally translated, of course, these terms are *form history* and *redaction history,* and these terms are sometimes employed; but "form and redaction *criticism*" is more conventionally established, albeit sometimes conceptually misleading. I think the literal translation more apt.

[2] Joseph B. Tyson, *A Study of Early Christianity,* New York, 1973, p. 164.

[3] "Gerald Ford's Joke Book," by Anne Beatts, *The Village Voice,* December 10, 1974, p. 7.

[4] Rudolf Bultmann, *The History of the Synoptic Tradition,* trans. John Marsh, Oxford, 1963, p. 4.

[5] Herald Riesenfeld, *The Gospel Tradition,* Philadelphia, 1970, p. 5.

[6] "The Study of the Synoptic Gospels" in *Form Criticism,* trans. Frederick C. Grant, New York, 1934, 1962, p. 32.

[7] Hans Conzelmann, *The Theology of St. Luke,* trans. Goeffrey Buswell, London, 1960, p. 10.

[8] "The Study of the Synoptic Gospels," in *Form Criticism,* p. 70.

[9] *Ibid.,* p. 70.

[10] Bultmann, *History,* p. 7.

[11] Henry Hogarth, "A New Look at Mark's Gospel," *Expository Times* 84 (1972), p. 88.

[12] T. A. Burkill, *Mysterious Revelation,*

Ithaca, 1963, p. 24—here agreeing with Austin Farrer in rejecting the quoted assessment of Mark.

[13]Morton S. Enslin, "The Artistry of Mark," *JBL* 66 (1947), pp. 392, 399.

[14]The methodological infelicity of the assumptions governing the prevailing approach seems to me aptly, if indeliberately, exposed by John Bowman, who writes that "It [Mark] is...highly stylized and rigorously subordinated to a certain pattern. But what pattern?" (*The Gospel of Mark*, Leiden, 1965, p. xiv). And, one may ask, what rigorous subordination?

[15]The reference to the wilderness obviously has theological import, at least through its conuunction with the Isaian quotation in 1:3. But Marxsen's claim that "the concept 'wilderness,' in itself geographical, is emptied of its geographical content" (Willi Marxsen, *Mark the Evangelist*, trans. James Boyce, *et al.*, Nashville, 1969, p.43 is simply without foundation. Such a geographical kenosis is a function of his finesse, not that of the Marcan text. As for the non-geographical dimension of its Marcan meaning, I cannot understand why Marxsen is willing to grant that the sea can "denote a solitary region" (p. 63) and is nevertheless unwilling, despite the obvious implications of 6:31, to allow the wilderness sometimes (e.g., 1:12) to have basically such a simple function.

[16]Marxsen unconsciously admits as much when he undermines his confident assurance that "this much appears to emerge with relative certainty: the diet points to a vegetarian ascetic; the clothing, and especially the leather girdle, to Elijah" by following it with the plausible hypothesis that "Perhaps in that day such a garb was required of a prophet" (*Mark the Evan-*

gelist, p. 36). If the latter is the case, the clothing points at most to prophetic character in general, not Elijah in particular—and it is just as likely that the clothing, like the diet, was understood to be simply that of an ascetic, period.

[17]Lohmeyer comments on the phrase, "dieser Satz scheint das Grauen verstärken zu sollen, das die Wüste als satanische Stätte ausatmet; denn die 'Tiere' sind des Satans Verbündete" (Ernst Lohmeyer, *Das Evangelium des Markus,* Göttingen, 1967, p. 27). A plausible guess; but the "zu sollen" is as judiciously chosen as the "scheint": if this was the intent, it was not achieved.

[18]Marxsen's steadfast denial of Mark's temporally sequential presentation—"the concept of time is, as it were, eliminated" (p. 42); "This arrangement, however, is in no way intended to express temporal sequence" (p. 43)—is a stance which the text simply will not support. (Nor will Marxsen himself support it unequivocally, for *cf.* his remark on p. 131: "Sequence, chronological order—all this is certainly in the material or is at least intended there...").

[19]The supposition that Mark is deliberately uninterested in such considerations for theological reasons is extremely difficult to reconcile with 6:17-29, as well as being dependent upon a willingness to infer a theological program from mainly negative—and inconsistent—evidences.

[20]If Mark were following Marxsen's theological scheme, he would be much more likely either to emphasize the *return* to Galilee, or to use a still more neutral word such as *egeneto.*

[21]For a fuller discussion on this crux, see Tj. Baarda, "Gadarenes, Garasenes,

Gergesenes and the 'Diatessaron' Traditions,"
*Neotestamentica et Semitica: Studies in Honour
of Matthew Black,* Edinburgh, 1969, pp. 181-197.

[22]For a representative example of the ways
in which those more generous and imaginative
than realistically critical have tried to follow Mark into the mystery, consider this: "Thus
the disciples ought to see the secret significance of the miracle of the loaves; that is to
say, they ought to understand what the evangelist
apparently means his readers to understand,
namely, that Jesus is none other than the Messiah and Lord, whose presence is discerned at
the church's sacramental meals of fellowship
and who imparts spiritual food for the nourish-
ment of the souls of the elect. To use termi-
nology derived from John 6:22 ff., he is the
bread of life which comes down from heaven and
the one true loaf that is with the disciples in
the ship" (T. A. Burkill, *op. cit.,* p. 107).
If Mark really meant his readers to understand
that his pericope means this, he gave them about
as much credit for miraculous inference as
Burkill gives Mark for miraculous implication.
But in fairness to Burkill, it must be acknowl-
edged that if one does not fault Mark in this
instance, one ought to go as far as Burkill does
in the other direction: otherwise, there is no
accounting for the fact that after Jesus has
cured and exorcised, and communicated to others
the power to do so, and taught new things au-
thoritatively, and raised the dead, and forgiven sins, and claimed rights over the Sabbath
with a self-justifying comparison with David,
and walked on water, it is nevertheless the incident of the *loaves* that is singled out as the
key to insight. (For the most thoroughgoing attempt to give Mark the benefit of such a procedural supposition on this matter, see Quentin
Quesnell, *The Mind of Mark,* Rome, 1969). Either
Mark sees and means to imply an extravagantly

great deal thereby, or he is mystified. If it
is the former, he has not given us much help to
follow him, and Burkill's kind of ingenuity with
the passage is indispensable. But weigh the
plausibilities. (For a more contemporary analogue, consider F. J. Sheed's description of an
ordinary Christian's explanation of the doctrine
of the Trinity: "From the believer's mouth there
emerges what can only be called a soup of words,
sentences that begin and do not end, words that
change into something else halfway. This goes
on for a longer or shorter time. But finally
there comes something like 'Thus, you see, three
is one and one is three.' The questioner not un-
naturally retorts that three is not one nor one
three. Then comes the believer's great moment.
With his eyes fairly gleaming he cries: 'Ah,
that is the mystery. You have to have faith'"
[*Theology and Sanity,* New York, 1946, p. 65]).

   [23] In addition to these instances of instruction on sayings which puzzled the disciples,
there are also the cases of the transfiguration
and the predictions of the passion; but these
are only analogues of the motif under discussion
rather than instances of it—at least in the form
in which Mark presents them, though they were undoubtedly once much closer.

   [24] The most plausible reconstruction of that
pre-Marcan tradition, to my mind, is that given
by T. W. Manson (*The Teaching of Jesus,* 2nd edition, Cambridge, 1935, pp. 75-80), and developed
by Matthew Black (*An Aramaic Approach to the
Gospels and Acts,* Third Edition, Oxford, 1967,
pp. 211-216), supplemented by the suggestion of
Joachim Jeremias (*The Parables of Jesus* [revised
edition], London, 1963): *viz.,* that its function
traditionally had been to describe Jesus' teaching in general, not the parables in particular.
But against Jeremias (p. 17) and Marxsen ("Redaktionsgeschichtliche Erklärung der sogenannten

Parabeltheorie des Markus," *ZTK* 52 (1955), p.
269), and with Black, I cannot see any adequate
ground for concluding that the benign construction given by Targum or Rabbinic commentary to
the Isaian text can legitimately be smuggled
past the stark Marcan wording by a benevolent
exegesis—even so subtle an exegesis as that offered by C. F. D. Moule, "Mark 4:1-20 Yet Once
More," in *Neotestamentica et Semitica,* pp. 95-113.

[25]Eduard Schweizer, "Zur Frage des Messiasgeheimnisses bei Markus," *ZNW* 56 (1965), pp. 1-8.

[26]Theodore   Weeden Jr., *Mark—Traditions in
Conflict,* Philadelphia, 1971, p. 140.

[27]*Ibid.,* p. 144.

[28]Marksen's ingenious explanation works
from the evangelist's own *Sitz im Leben* and refers the parable-theory crux to the Christian
perception of Jesus Christ as the Mystery of the
Kingdom (as against the hard-hearted opacity of
unbelievers): "*Jetzt* liegt das Messiasgeheimnis
vor, und zwar in der Verküdigung! Ihr Inhalt
ist das *mustērion,* das der Gemeinde offenbart
wird und denen draussen ein Rätsel bleibt" (Marxsen, "Redaktionsgeschichtliche Erklärung," p. 270).
But this interpretation seems to me neither in-
vited by the text nor indeed readily tolerated
by it. It seems to me simply incredible that
the evangelist should undertake to suggest so
subtle an insight by such a misleading and un-
accommodating procedure. The theory proposed by
Schweizer and developed by Weeden (*cf.* also J. W.
Pryor in *Expository Times* 83, 1972, pp. 242-245)
at least faces the inconsistency.

[29]*Cf.* the carefully intelligent, but similarly vulnerable, interpretation of David J.
Hawkins, "The Incomprehension of the Disciples
in the Marcan Redaction," *JBL* 91 (1972), pp. 491-
500.

[30]Despite the resignation of Jeremias to
the conclusion that the interpretation of the
parable "must be ascribed to the primitive
Church" (Jeremias, *op. cit.*, p. 77), I do not
find his linguistic argument persuasive (pp.
77-8), since it stratifies the usages of the
first century too neatly. I see no reason to
be sure that parable and explication were not
linked together from the days of Jesus' earthly
ministry. (*Cf.* Moule, *op. cit.*, pp. 106-113).
At any rate, the explanation is not Mark's invention, as Jeremias observes (p. 79), and thus
must have come to *him* already linked to the
parable—and presumably without the break and
scene-change which his Gospel places between
them.

[31]The first of these passages is given
from the RSV; the second is my own translation
from the LXX; the third is as rendered by Matthew Black, *An Aramaic Approach*, p. 214.

[32]*An Aramaic Approach,* pp. 211-216.

[33]The Targum was, like the general tradi-
tion of Targumic renditions of Scripture in the
Synagogue, not a mere translation but an inter-
pretive gloss; see S. Safrai and M. Stern, eds.,
The Jewish People in the First Century, vol. 2,
Assen, 1976, p. 1032.

[34]*An Aramaic Approach,* p. 215.

[35]Mark's summary observation in 4:34 is
not found in Matthew or Luke. I assume that if
it is not entirely Mark's invention, he has at
least readjusted it to conform with the kind of
private explication he presents.

[36]Evidently, the presentation of such
teachings by the route of explicated parables,
despite its congenial affinities with the motif
of esoteric revelation popular in apocalyptic

circles (for which, see Erik Sjoberg, *Der Verborgene Menschensohn in den Evangelien,* Lund,
1955), seemed eventually to compromise it too
much. It was accordingly detached from the
parables and presented in summary form more directly. But the traditional memory of esoteric
explication did not vanish immediately when this
literary readjustment removed its objective
ground: thus the vacuum which Mark or his tradition ingeniously, if misleadingly, fill with a
further readjustment.

BIBLIOGRAPHY

Ambrozic, Aloysius M. *The Hidden Kingdom*. Washington, D.C., 1972.

Anne, David E. "The Problem of the Messianic Secret in Mark." *Novum Testamentum*, 11 (1969), 1-31.

Baarda, Tj. "Gaderenes, Garasenes, Gergesenes and the 'Diatessaron' Traditions." *Neotestamentica et Semitica: Studies in Honour of Matthew Black*. Edinburgh, 1969, 181-97.

Baird, A. "A Pragmatic Approach to Parable Exegesis: Some New Evidence on Mk 4,11.34-34." *Journal of Biblical Literature*, 76 (1957), 201-07.

Black, Matthew. *An Aramaic Approach to the Gospels and Acts*. 3rd ed. Oxford, 1967.

Boobyer, G. H. "The Redaction of Mk 4, 1-34." *New Testament Studies*, 8 (1961-62), 59-70.

Bowman, John. *The Gospel of Mark*. Leiden, 1965.

Bultmann, Rudolf. *Form Criticism*. Trans. F. C. Grant. New York, 1934.

_____. *The History of the Synoptic Tradition*. Trans. John Marsh. Oxford, 1963.

Burkill, T. A. *Mysterious Revelation*. Ithaca, 1963.

Conzelmann, Hans. *The Theology of St. Luke*. Trans. Goeffrey Buswell. London, 1960.

Coutts, J. "Those Outside (Mk 4, 10-12)." *Studia Evangelica*, 2 (1963), 155-57.

Daube, David. *The Sudden in Scripture*. Leiden, 1964.

_____. "Public Pronouncement and Private Ex-
    planation in the Gospels." *Expository Times,*
    57 (1946), 175-77.

Dodd, C. H. *Parables of the Kingdom.* New York,
    1961.

Elliot, J. K. *"Ho baptizōn* and Mk 1, 4." *Theo-
    logische Zeitschrift,* 31 (1975), 14-15.

Enslin, Morton. "The Artistry of Mark." *Journal
    of Biblical Literature,* 66 (1947), 385-99.

Farmer, William E. *The Synoptic Problem.* New York,
    1964.

Feuillet, A. "L'historicité des récits évangélique
    du baptême de Jésus." *Nova et Vetera,* 52
    (1977), 178-87.

Freyne, Sean. *The Twelve: Disciples and Apostles.*
    London, 1968.

Gerhardsson, Birger. "The Parable of the Sower and
    Its Interpretation." *New Testament Studies,*
    14 (1968), 165-93.

Gero, S. "The Spirit as a Dove at the Baptism of
    Jesus." *Novum Testamentum,* 18 (1976), 17-35.

Gnilka, Joachim. *Die Verstockung Israels. Isaiah
    6, 9-10 in der Theologie der Synoptiker.* Munic
    1961.

Grobel, K. "He That Cometh After Me." *Journal of
    Biblical Literature,* 60 (1941), 397-401.

Haenchen, Ernst. *Der Weg Jesu.* Berlin, 1966.

Hammer, R. "Elijah and Jesus: A Quest for Identity
    Journal of Biblical Literature, 19 (1970),
    207-18.

Hawkins, David J. "The Incomprehension of the

Disciples in the Markan Redaction." *Journal of Biblical Literature,* 91 (1972), 491-500.

Hengel, Martin. *Nachfolge und Charisma.* Berlin, 1968.

Hogarth, Henry. "A New Look at Mark's Gospel." *Expository Times,* 84 (1972), 88-90.

Jeremias, Joachim. *The Parables of Jesus.* London, 1963.

Jäuon, Paul. "Le costume d'Elie et celui de Jean Baptiste." *Biblica,* 16 (1935), 74-81.

Johnson, Sherman E. *A Commentary on the Gospel According to St. Mark.* 2nd ed. London, 1972.

Jones, G. V. *The Art and Truth of the Parables.* London, 1964.

Kee, Howard C. *Community of the New Age.* Philadelphia, 1977.

Kelber, W. H. *The Kingdom in Mark.* Philadelphia, 1974.

Kertelege, K. *Die Wunder Jesu im Markusevangelium.* Munich, 1970.

Kuhn, Heinz-Wolfgang. *Ältere Sammlungen im Markusevangelium.* Göttingen, 1971.

Lagrance, M.-J. *Evangile selon Saint Jean.* Paris, 1936.

Lohmeyer, Ernst. *Das Evangelium des Markus.* Göttingen, 1967.

Manson, T. W. *The Teaching of Jesus.* 2nd ed. Cambridge, 1935.

Marxsen, Willi. *Mark the Evangelist.* Trans. James Boyce et al. Nashville, 1969.

_____.   "Redaktionsgeschichtliche Erklaru
    des sogenannten Parabeltheorie des Markus."
    Zeitschrift für Theologie und Kirche, 52 (195
    255-71.

Mauser, U. *Christ in the Wilderness*. London, 1963

Meye, Robert P. "Mark 4, 10: Those About Him With
    the Twelve." *Studia Evangelia*, 2 (1963), 211
    18.

Mosley, A. W. "Jesus' Audiences in the Gospels of
    St. Mark and St. Luke." *New Testament Studie*
    10 (1963-64), 139-49.

Moule, C. F. D. "Mark 4, 1-20 Yet Once More."
    Neotestamentica et Semitica: Studies in Honou
    of Matthew Black. Edinburgh, 1969, 95-113.

Nineham, D. E. *Saint Mark*. London, 1973.

Pesch, R. *Das Markusevangelium*. Vol. 1. Freiburg
    1976.

Pryor, J. W. "Markan Parable Theology." *Exposito*
    Times, 83 (1972), 242-45.

Quesnell, Quentin. *The Mind of Mark*. Rome, 1969.

Richter, G. "Zu den Tauferzählungen Mk 1, 9-11
    und Jn 1, 32-34." *Zeitschrift für Neutestame*
    lische Wissenschaft, 65 (1974), 43-56.

Riesenfeld, Harald. *The Gospel Tradition*. Phila-
    delphia, 1970.

Robinson, J. A. T. "Elijah, John and Jesus: An Es
    say in Detection." *New Testament Studies*, 4
    (1957-58), 263-81.

_____. *Studies in Mark's Gospel*. Nashville,
    1958.

Ruddick, C. T. "Behold I Send My Messenger." *Jou*
    nal of Biblical Literature, 88 (1969), 381-41

Safrai, S. and Stern, M., eds. *The Jewish People in the First Century.* 2 vols. Assen, 1976.

Schmid, J. *The Gospel According to Mark.* Trans. Kevin Condon. Staten Island, 1968.

Schulz, A. *Nachfolgen und Nachahmen.* Munich, 1962.

Schweizer, Eduard. "Anmerkungen zur Theologie des Markus." *Neotestamentica.* Zurich, 1963.

_____. *Das Evangelium nach Markus.* Göttingen, 1967.

_____. "Ökumene im Neuen Testament: Der Glaube an den Sohn Gottes." *Beiträge zur Theologie des Neuen Testament 1955-1970.* Zurich, 1970.

Schweizer, Eduard. "Zur Frage des Messiasgeheimnisses bei Markus." *Zeitschrift für Neutestamentliche Wissenschaft,* 56 (1965), 1-8.

Sheed, F. J. *Theology and Sanity.* New York, 1946.

Sjoberg, Erik. *Der Verborgene Menschensohn in den Evangelien.* Lund, 1955.

Smith, Morton. "Comments on Taylor's Commentary on Mark." *Harvard Theological Review,* 48 (1955), 21-64.

Stein, Robert H. "The Proper Methodology for Ascertaining a Marcan Redaction History." *Novum Testamentum,* 13 (1971), 181-198.

Swete, Henry Barclay. *The Gospel According to St. Mark.* London, 1898.

Taylor, Vincent P. *The Gospel According to Saint Mark.* London, 1952.

Trocmé, Etienne. *The Formation of the Gospel According to Mark.* Trans. Pamela Gaughan. Philadelphia, 1975.

Tyson, Joseph B.   *A Study of Early Christianity.*
       New York, 1973.

Vielhauer, P.   "Erwägungen zur Christologie des
       Markusevangeliums."   *Zeit und Geschichte.*   Ed
       Erich Dinkler. Tübingen, 1964,   155-70.

_____.   "Tracht und Speise Johannes des Taufers
       Aufsätze zum Neuen Testament. Munich, 1965.

Weeden, Theodore Jr.   *Mark--Traditions in Conflict.*
       Philadelphia, 1971.

White, K. D.   "The Parable of the Sower."   *Journal
       of Theological Studies,* n.s.   15 (1964), 300-

Windisch, H.   "Die Notiz über Tracht und Speise de
       Taufers Johannes und ihre Entsprechungen in d
       Jesusüberlieferung."   *Zeitschrift für Neutes-
       tamentliche Wissenschaft,* 32 (1933), 65-87.

Wrede, D. W.   *Das Messiasgeheimnis in den Evangeli*
       Göttingen, 1901.

BIBLICAL INDEX